THE ANCIENT COMEDIANS

ALSO BY CLEM MARTINI

On playwriting
The Blunt Playwright
The Greek Playwright

Drama
The Field Mouse Collection
Illegal Entry
Martini With A Twist
A Three Martini Lunch

Young adult fiction
The Crow Chronicles (The Mob, The Plague, The Judgment)
Too Late

Graphic novels (with Olivier Martini)
Bitter Medicine: A Graphic Memoir of Mental Illness

THE ANCIENT COMEDIANS

AND WHAT THEY HAVE TO SAY TO CONTEMPORARY PLAYWRIGHTS

CLEM MARTINI

PLAYWRIGHTS CANADA PRESS
TORONTO

Excerpts from *Greek And Roman Comedy: Translations And Interpretations Of Four Representative Plays*, edited by Shawn O'Bryhim, Copyright © 2001 by Shawn O'Bryhim and reprinted with the permission of the University of Texas Press.

Excerpts from *Menander: The Plays and Fragments*, translated by Maurice Balme, Copyright © 2001 by Maurice Balme and used by permission of Oxford University Press.

Excerpts from *Aristophanes: Four Comedies*, edited by William Arrowsmith, Copyright © 1969 by William Arrowsmith and reprinted with the permission of the University of Michigan Press.

Excerpts from pages 100, 108–109, 207, and 215–219 of *Plautus: The Comedies*, edited by David R. Slavitt and Palmer Bovie, Copyright © 1995 by The Johns Hopkins University Press and reprinted with permission of Johns Hopkins University Press.

LIBRARY AND ARCHIVES CANADA CATALOGUING IN PUBLICATION
Martini, Clem, 1956-, author
      The ancient comedians : and what they have to say to contemporary playwrights
/ Clem Martini.

ISBN 978-1-77091-273-1 (pbk.)

      1. Greek drama (Comedy)--History and criticism. 2. Latin drama
(Comedy)--History and criticism. 3. Comedy--Greek influences.
4. Comedy--Roman influences. I. Title.

PA3028.M37 2014   882'.0109   C2014-904140-3

We acknowledge the financial support of the Canada Council for the Arts, the Ontario Arts Council (OAC), the Ontario Media Development Corporation, and the Government of Canada through the Canada Book Fund for our publishing activities.

 Canada Council   Conseil des arts
for the Arts   du Canada

 ONTARIO ARTS COUNCIL
CONSEIL DES ARTS DE L'ONTARIO
an Ontario government agency
un organisme du gouvernement de l'Ontario

 Canadä

 Ontario
Ontario Media Development
Corporation

To comedians, past and present—
what a dreary world it would be
without them.

TABLE OF CONTENTS

PREFACE   V

INTRODUCTION   VII

COMIC TENDENCIES   X

1. THE EVOLUTION OF COMEDY   1

2. THE COMEDIANS   6
   I. THE GREEKS   8
   II. THE ROMANS   15

3. CONFLICT, OR PICKING YOUR FIGHTS   23

4. A WORLD TURNED UPSIDE DOWN—THE REMARKABLE
PROPERTIES OF THE FORBIDDEN, UNEXPECTED, AND
INAPPROPRIATE   28
   I. THE UNEXPECTED   28
   II. THE FORBIDDEN   30
   III. INAPPROPRIATENESS OF RESPONSE,
   OR DOING IT WRONG   34

5. RELENTLESS OVERWHELMING BUSYNESS OF
THE PROTAGONIST   40

6. THE UTILITY OF A GOOD VILLAIN   47

7. POLITICS, STATUS, HIERARCHY, AND COMEDY   59

8. ROMANCE AS A CREATIVE CRUCIBLE   70

9. CONFLICT IN ACTION—COMEDY AND VIOLENCE   77

10. SEXUALITY AND COMEDY IN THE THEATRE   86

11. VISUAL COMEDY   95

12. THE POETICS OF COMEDY   101
   I. FIGURES OF SPEECH AND PLAYFUL LANGUAGE   102
   II. THE RUNNING GAG   104

III. DIRECT ADDRESS AND THE PARABASIS   109
IV. MULTIPLE PLOTS   113
V. MUSICALITY   117

CONCLUSION   119
APPENDIX A—TIMELINE OF THE DEVELOPMENT OF COMEDIC THEATRE   125
APPENDIX B—SYNOPSES   128
BIBLIOGRAPHY/RECOMMENDED WORKS   147

PREFACE

In *The Blunt Playwright* I wrote, "The subject of comedy is so immense that any serious analysis of it could take up a book all on its own." Let's be clear, *The Ancient Comedians* is not that book.

Over time, there have been a number of scholars from various disciplines who have weighed in on the topic of comic theory, some with greater success than others. The esteemed English philosopher Thomas Hobbes, for instance, wrote, "Sudden glory is the passion which maketh those grimaces called laughter; and is caused either by some sudden act of their own, that pleaseth them; or by the apprehension of some deformed thing in another, by comparison whereof they suddenly applaud themselves."[1] Renowned psychoanalyst Dr. Sigmund Freud suggested that "a person appears comic to us, if in comparison with ourselves, he makes too great an expenditure on his bodily functions and too little on his mental ones, and it cannot be denied that in both these cases our laughter expresses a pleasurable sense of the superiority which we feel in relation to him."[2] German philosopher Immanuel Kant summarized comedy as "the sudden perception of the incongruity between a concept and real objects which have been thought through in some relation, and laughter itself is just the expression of this incongruity."[3] And French literary theorist Henri-Louis Bergson wrote that comedy resulted from repetition and mechanical

---

1   Thomas Hobbes, *Leviathan*, bk. 1, chap. 6 (Project Gutenberg, 2009). www.gutenberg.org/files/3207/3207-h/3207-h.htm.

2   Sigmund Freud, "Jokes and the Comic," in *Jokes and Their Relation to the Unconscious*, ed. and trans. James Strachey (New York: W.W. Norton, 1960), 45.

3   Qtd. in James Kern Feibleman, *In Praise of Comedy: A Study in Its Theory and Practice* (New York: Russell and Russell, 1962), 109.

inelasticity, or, as he put it so succinctly, when there is "something mechanical encrusted on the living."[4]

In the end—at least for the playwright—I believe the study of comedy isn't so much a science as it is a practice, and I'm not sure that delving into involved analytical theories is particularly helpful. If you wish to ride a unicycle, it may be less useful to perform detailed studies of the physics of motion than to consult with someone who has actually mounted a unicycle and learned how to make it go.

So, if you wish to unlock the secrets of why humans laugh, Bergson, Hobbes, Freud, or Kant may be who you wish to consult, but if you are thinking about the ancient Greek and Roman comic playwrights and wondering how it's possible that they created plays thousands of years ago that are still funny and produceable today, or, if you are interested in writing comedy and feel that there may be things to learn from those who first wrote in that form—this may be your book.

The decisions those playwrights made, and the plays they wrote, may be important ones to consider.

---

4   Henri Bergson, *Laughter*, trans. Cloudesley Shovell Henry Brereton and Fred Rothwell (New York: Macmillan, 1928), 37.

INTRODUCTION

So what *do* the ancient playwrights have to say to contemporary play-wrights? In a culture as essentially future-oriented as the one we live in today, why might it be useful and interesting to examine the works of dead poets?

There is a canon of about thirty-eight more-or-less intact comic plays written by the early Greek and Roman comic playwrights. (See Appendix B for a synopsis of each play.) These plays, written so long ago, are still studied and performed after two thousand years. That's a very credible run. They have been enormously influential on what we, today, consider funny, and how we create, produce, and process comedy in the theatre. In his text on the long-lasting impact of Plautus and Terence, Robert Miola claims that

> employing the biological metaphor, we can say that the plays of Plautus and Terence, themselves descendants of barely visible forebears, engendered countless progeny, including works by Hrosvit, Ariosto, Berrardo, Trissino, Cecchi, Dolce, Delia Porta, Machiavelli, Turnèbe, Garnier, Grévin, Jodelle, Belleau, Larivey, Rotrou, Baïf, La Taille, Molière, Rueda, Molina, Vega, Calderón, Heywood, Shakespeare, Jonson, Middleton, Congreve, Farquhar, Wycherley, Sheridan, Wilde, and Shaw. Mixing freely with the bloodlines of other traditions, appearing in various productions, translations, and refigurations, Plautus and Terence bequeathed to posterity the essential genetic make-up of their genre, dramatic comedy.[1]

1   Robert S. Miola, *Shakespeare and Classical Comedy: The Influence of Plautus and Terence* (Oxford Scholarship Online, 2011). www.oxfordscholarship.com/view/10.1093/acprof:oso/9780198182696.001.0001/acprof-9780198182696?rskey=WRLpsx&result=1.

Statue representing a comic mask, outside the Theatre of Ostia near Rome.

If you are interested in writing comedy, many of the strategies employed to generate comedic plays were first developed by these early playwrights. They thought deeply about how to entertain an audience, focus and sustain their attention, and make them laugh. The more one considers the tools that were developed thousands of years ago, the more it becomes apparent that those same skills still have application today.

Nevertheless, if this book isn't meant to be an analysis of comedy, neither is it intended to be a "how-to" book. I believe nothing quite so prescriptive is desirable or even possible. If you do as the ancient comedians did there can be no guarantee that you will suddenly, miraculously, knock off a successful comedy. There are no miraculous formulas, modern or ancient, that will endow any art form with success. The works of Aristophanes, Plautus, Terence, and Menander offer ideas to contemplate, not blueprints to execute.

If you have already read the ancient Greeks and Romans and enjoyed their plays, you won't need me to trumpet their many intrinsic virtues— the energetic sense of humour and spirit of invention they manifest, the wit and wordplay they display, the feelings for humanity that they evoke—but it may be necessary to present a final caveat. One has to note that the Greeks and Romans are not perfect role models. In fact, they are highly, flamboyantly imperfect. They were nothing if not products of their times, and the societies in which they were raised were seriously flawed and fractious. The plays—mirroring the society they lived in—are violent and feature institutionalized slavery, sexism, and gratuitous obscenity and vulgarity. Furthermore, they rely on cheap jokes and bad puns.

But, if you are prepared to suspend censure of those elements that arose from the times in which they lived, there is much to admire in the iconoclastic nature of the comedy they created. The writers of antiquity were neither rebels nor revolutionaries, but it is the nature of comedy to respond to power and privilege and so imbedded within the narratives are commentaries, critiques, and attacks—subtle and not so subtle—on hierarchical institutions and individuals holding authority.

And who can possibly object to cheap jokes and bad puns?

COMIC TENDENCIES

Every philosopher has his try at a definition of laughter
and, according to Jean Paul Richter, the sole merit of all
the definitions was to be themselves comic. For the comic
is not demonstrable, it climbs no staircase into conscious-
ness, but flies instead, through the window, instantly, like
sunlight into a darkened chamber when we raise the blind.
And, like the sunlight, it eludes the grasping hand.
—Willard Mallalieu Smith,
The Nature of Comedy

I said this book wouldn't attempt to provide an analysis of comedy—and
it won't—but if there is to be agreement about what constitutes successful
comic strategies, there must first be agreement about what can be considered appropriate comic goals.

These, then, are six commonalities, or comic tendencies, that are neither
rules nor intended to be exclusive. There may be other comic propensi-
ties—these are just some of the more common ones.

1. *Comedy is an imitation* in the same way that tragedy
is an imitation—of life. As Aristotle wrote in his *Poetics*,
"Now epic-making and the making of tragedy, and comedy
too, and the art of making dithyrambs, and most of the art
of composing to the flute and lyre—all these happen to be,
by and large, *mimeseis*."[1] Both forms, Aristotle asserted,
observe life, and then extrapolate from that observation.
Both forms declare life is like *this*. So, both rely upon the

1   Aristotle, *Aristotle's Poetics*, trans. George Whalley, ed. John Baxter (Montreal:
McGill-Queen's UP, 1997), 82.

quality and detail of the observations made by the artist. Even when a writer works against the grain and presents an absurd or a fantastical setting, the comedy relies upon the device of responding to a recognizable world in order to proclaim its difference.

2. *Comedy is active.* If one is to understand something as laughable, it is necessary to first witness the ridiculous, absurd, comical activity. Or as writer Willard Smith says, "Comedy is character in action, and... the comic is the informing spirit of that action."[2]

3. The comic silent film star, Charlie Chaplin, commented that "comedy is life viewed from a distance; tragedy, life in a close-up,"[3] and I believe there is something in *comedy that has something to do with alternative perspectives.* If things are habitually viewed one way, comedy proposes that they be viewed in another. Viewed from the perspective of the servant. Viewed from the perspective of the person fallen from power. Viewed from the perspective of the glutton or the miser or the voluptuary. Comedy loves perspectives that arise out of the exchanging of roles and positions. It glories in the high brought low, and low elevated on high.

4. *Comedy often relies upon exaggeration.* It exaggerates circumstances, it inflates aspects of character, it promotes violence that is larger than normal, lust that is more lustful, evil that is more wicked. Something about comedy tends to depend upon scale, and certainly this comic exaggeration can be found in the writing of the ancients. As George Duckworth observes in *The Nature of Roman Comedy*

---

2   Willard Mallalieu Smith, *The Nature of Comedy* (Boston: Gorham Press, 1930), 11.

3   Harry Levin, *Playboys and Killjoys: An Essay on the Theory and Practice of Comedy* (Toronto: Oxford UP, 1988), 9.

when discussing comic "elements," "Chief among these devices is that of exaggeration."[4]

5. *Comedy tends to rely upon speed.* A comic play tends to be a quick play. Perhaps there is something about the audience being surprised by an idea before it can determine its ultimate destination. This, after all, is the notion behind the comic punchline—swift delivery and sudden epiphany. The comic writer, Goldoni, reflected on this when he noted that his audiences "demand... that the plot be fairly rich in surprises and novelties... They want an unexpected ending."[5] If you present an idea slowly, it lends itself to rational analysis. If you present the idea quickly, it lends itself to surprise, shock, the sense of seeing things anew, and potentially, at least, amusement.

6. Finally, *comedy tends to resist suffering and relies upon physical and emotional resilience.* This is perhaps the element that most differentiates comedy from tragedy. Not everything in comedy is light. Violence occurs, evil is encountered, heartbreak happens, but unlike in tragic plays where things are left shattered and hearts remain fractured, comedy tends to mend. Comic heroes bounce back. In his *Poetics*, Aristotle makes the distinction clear when he writes, "Comedy is, as we said, a mimesis of inferior persons—not however that it has to do with the whole [range of] wickedness but with what is funny—an aspect of ugliness. A funny thing, to be precise, is a clumsy mistake that is not painful or destructive: [or] to take an obvious example, the comic mask is ugly and grotesque but not repulsive or painful."[6]

---

4   George E. Duckworth, *The Nature of Roman Comedy*, 2nd ed. (Norman: U of Oklahoma P, 1994), 321.

5   Qtd. in Andrew Calder, *Molière: The Theory and Practice of Comedy* (London: Continuum, 2000), 19.

6   Aristotle, 63.

The differences become more obvious with specific comparisons. In *Oedipus Tyrannus*, Oedipus discovers his complicity in the curse, blinds himself, and stumbles into exile; in Plautus's play *The Two Bacchides*, the comic slave Chrysalus is tied up, beaten, and threatened with worse violence, but ultimately is released and walks away happily and successfully (see Chapter 9 for a portion of this scene).

1. THE EVOLUTION OF COMEDY

Nobody invented a sense of humour.

That—happily—appears to be an intrinsic part of the human condition and we all enter the world equipped with the ability to laugh. What the Greeks did first, and the Romans did after, was develop and refine ways to express that comic sensibility in the theatre. It was the first comic literature of Western civilization that was shared broadly. The theatre, based upon written scripts, permitted fictional stories to be presented in a precise, consistent manner, reflecting not only the content of the narrative itself but also the individual style of its authors.

How comedy developed, and who precisely participated in the development is somewhat obscured by time. In his *Poetics*, Aristotle lays out his general impressions on how comedy in the theatre evolved.

> Because comedy was not taken seriously at first, it is only after it had already to some extent taken shape that there is a record of people called "comic poets." (In fact the archon did not give a chorus to comic poets until quite late on, before that, the chorus were volunteers.) Indeed [comedy] already had certain distinctive features by the time "comic" poets came along and were recorded. Who supplied masks or prologues or companies of actors is not known. But the constructing of plots came from Sicily originally, and in Athens it was Crates who first abandoned the "iambic" and began to make stories—that is, plots—in a typical way.[1]

---

1   Aristotle, *Aristotle's Poetics*, trans. George Whalley, ed. John Baxter (Montreal: McGill-Queen's UP, 1997), 100.

Some believe, and certainly Aristotle suggests this as a possibility, that comedy sprang out of a tradition of lampooning that existed in the Greek rural communities. There is evidence of this by way of art, illustrations on a variety of ancient vases depicting some kind of potentially comic activity in which individuals dressed in padded costumes and animal skins dance. Some feel that the development of comedy may have been closely connected to what we know of as the Satyr plays, works based on a mythological theme that normally accompanied the trilogy of tragedies performed during the Festival of the Greater Dionysia. How any of these activities precisely align with the development of comic theatre is uncertain.

In any case, we know that by 486 BCE comic plays were written and presented as part of a religious ceremony honouring Dionysus in Athens. During the Greater Dionysia and the Lenaian festivals, scripts would be selected, choruses would be awarded, and following a period of rehearsal, the plays were presented in competition with one another. The only examples of the comic scripts produced in those earliest days are those written by Aristophanes. His plays, and—if we can extrapolate from those plays and the incomplete fragments of other scripts—the plays of that time, can generally be characterized as being political, satirical, bawdy, musical, and requiring a large number of well-rehearsed chorus members to speak, sing, and dance the narrative.

As the political situation of Athens changed, so did the theatre. Athens had embarked upon building an empire, which collapsed when Athens lost the war of attrition that it had waged for decades (431–404 BCE) with nearby city state, Sparta. Democracy was dissolved and Athens was occupied. Comic plays at this point—perhaps because of the risk involved in poking fun at those in power—began to refrain from offering political commentary. Love stories and plays exploring familial relationships grew in popularity.

By the mid-fourth century BCE, theatre had evolved in significant ways. Comedies were less reliant upon choruses and more reliant upon clear representations of character, were less political and satirical in tone, and more firmly connected to a formal narrative plot. This is deduced from commentary of a variety of ancient scholars, and from the few examples that remain. Beyond the less-than-complete fragments, the only intact surviving play we have from this period is *Dyskolos* (*The Grouch*), written by Menander. A number of Menander's plays, and those of his contemporaries, were later adapted into Latin by Romans, however, so those examples exist as well. More about them later.

The style of theatre was necessarily evolving, and with it the mechanism of delivery. Theatre had been planted and taken root wherever Alexander the Great had conquered and colonized. The Hellenistic Period (323–31 BCE) immediately following the death of Alexander the Great saw the rise of the great Technati: touring performance groups that travelled widely and delivered theatre throughout the Hellenized world. These powerful acting guilds—the Artists Guild of Dionysus, the Isthmian-Nemean Guild, and the Peloponnesian Guild, among others—were competitive, highly influential, and well-organized performance troupes. In addition to travelling and performing plays, they presided over a number of religious rituals and held the nearly autonomous status of a state. On the development of these guilds, Professor F.W. Walbank writes, "They were the product on the one hand of demand, for as the taste for Attic-style drama spread through the Greek culture area in the fourth and third century BCE it transformed festivals, stimulated the building of theatres, and thereby

The Cave of the Nymphs, near Syracuse, at one time headquarters of the actors guilds.

offered the means of existence to travelling actors, whether star players or whole companies."[2]

Overlapping with the spread of Greek theatre was the burgeoning of a major new international power. The Romans emerged as a powerful militarized city state and embarked on the establishment of their own empire. As the Romans stretched out, first from the city of Rome into peninsular Italy, and then subsequently further afield to the countries bordering the Mediterranean, they encountered and subsumed the former empire of the Greeks and Macedonians. In so doing, they adopted a great deal of the former empire's cultural infrastructure. Greek architecture and art, philosophy and medicine, were widely emulated in Rome.

The Romans were conflicted in their response to Greek culture, however. They both admired its sophistication and were intensely suspicious of its corrupting influence at the same time. Although the Romans began to adapt and produce versions of the Greek comedies, and although the Greeks had already built significant permanent theatres in what is now southern Italy, it was several hundred years before Roman authorities permitted their citizens to construct a permanent stone theatre. Up to that time, plays—though they were written and staged within the Roman Republic—were performed on temporary wooden structures that were erected specifically for certain religious festivals, and then demolished immediately after.

The earliest comic plays created by a Roman that we have in our possession today are those written by Titus Maccius Plautus (Plautus). As far as we know (not all source materials have been found) all of the plays written by Plautus were adaptations of works originally written by Greeks, and they were performed on these temporary, purpose-built wooden stages. Publius Terentius Afer (Terence) came onto the scene shortly after Plautus and continued in the tradition of his forebear, "turning" Greek plays to a Roman sensibility. His writing was not as exuberantly comic as that of Plautus. His plays were less violent, less bawdy, less musical, but they were more elegantly written, and the characters more realistically rendered.

As the Roman Republic evolved into the Roman Empire, the works of Plautus and Terence continued to be performed, but perhaps because

---

2   F.W. Walbank, *The Cambridge Ancient History*, vol. 7, part 1 (Cambridge: Cambridge UP, 1984), 319.

of the volatility of the times and emotional temperament of the various emperors, theatre became too risky to create and fewer new comedies were written. When the Roman Empire finally collapsed, the theatre withered as well, but the plays of Aristophanes, Menander, Plautus, and Terence quietly found a new audience, this time among the monastic scribes of the Middle Ages, who employed the texts for teaching Latin. These monks hand-copied the scripts and circulated them among the various religious centres. As a result of their efforts, these texts would survive and would later be read, studied, and imitated by subsequent generations of artists, such as Calderón, Shakespeare, and Molière. (A short timeline of the development of comedic theatre is included in the latter portions of this book.)

2. THE COMEDIANS

Who were these ancient comedians?

There are essentially four figures, two Greek and two Roman, who merit special attention. Why these four? As touched upon earlier, it is not necessarily because they were the very best of their craft—although they were certainly masters of their craft, and acknowledged as such in their times—it is simply that their scripts have survived. We have no way of comparing their works to those of their contemporaries because we do not possess any other comedic scripts of their time. As Shawn O'Bryhim notes, "There were other authors who probably wrote significantly different—and perhaps better—plays than the ones presented... but their works have been lost."[1]

Because the works of only these few celebrated figures survive, it is easy to believe that comedy was practised and enjoyed by the few. Not so. As David Roselli notes in his book, *Theater of the People*, "It cannot be stressed enough that the ancient theater was wildly popular."[2] In fact, comedy in ancient Greece and Rome had a long and robust history. Comic theatre was being written in the early sixth century BCE in Greece and continued to be created and produced until well into the development of the Roman Empire. You have only to visit those sites colonized by the ancient Greeks and Romans and see just how many theatres still exist to understand how vibrant the form once was. Professor Eric Csapo goes so far as to maintain that "drama became the primary vehicle of cultural Hellenization. West Greek pottery shows that by the last quarter of the fifth century the Greek colonists of Southern Italy had a close familiarity

---

1   Shawn O'Bryhim, *Greek and Roman Comedy: Translations and Interpretations of Four Representative Plays* (Austin: U of Texas P, 2001), viii.

2   David Kawalko Roselli, *Theater of the People: Spectators and Society in Ancient Athens* (Austin: U of Texas P, 2011), 21.

with Attic tragedy."[3] He is, of course, referencing Greek theatre, but this was equally true in terms of the robust dissemination of Roman comic theatre throughout the Roman Empire. There were many writers, and many scripts generated.

How is it possible that a form that thrived for hundreds of years left so few scripts behind? It's important to recall that there were comparatively few copies of the individual scripts to begin with. No mechanism of mass publication existed at the time. The scripts existed on scrolls of papyrus, and loosely bound "books," and these were all painstakingly copied out by hand.

Storage of written material was a highly imperfect practice. Scrolls were packed into vases or stacked on shelves and stored in private libraries or cellars. But when wars swept through a country, as they often did back in the day, libraries might have been looted or destroyed. Flooding could do great damage to written materials. Plays written on dry papyrus and brittle vellum made for excellent kindling. The great library at Alexandria held thousands of important scrolls, most of which were ultimately lost to fire. That any scripts survived at all was simply a matter of the most arbitrary chance.

---

3   Eric Csapo, *Actors and Icons of the Ancient Theater* (Hoboken, NJ: Wiley-Blackwell, 2010), 38.

I. THE GREEKS

The Theatre of Dionysus, site of many of the earliest Greek tragic and comic works.

ARISTOPHANES
446–386 BCE

It is my firm belief that Aristophanes stands with history's finest inspired artists, and that his poems are truth-disclosing works that speak to us thoughtfully as well as dramatically across the centuries.

—Bernard Freydberg,
Philosophy and Comedy

Aristophanes is the most widely known comic playwright of ancient Athens. As mentioned earlier, his are the only plays that have survived from the period known as Old Comedy. He was immensely popular in his own time, and has found fans throughout the passage of history. Even the very serious eminent German philosopher Hegel had a kind word to say about Aristophanes: "If you have not read him, you can scarcely realize how thoroughly jolly men can be."[4]

Possibly[5] born in Aegina, he lived the majority of his life in Athens, and wrote plays that were presented at the Athenian festivals and the Greater Dionysia and the Lenaian Festival. He was considered by his contemporaries to be a remarkably clever writer and an immensely talented poet. He began writing as a young person. *The Banqueters*, his first play, may have been produced when he was only eighteen, and *The Acharnians* was awarded first place at the Lenaian Festival in 425 BCE, when he was twenty-one. He was highly (famously) opinionated. His ideas were provocative—he excoriated the leaders of his day, wrote plays championing peace initiatives during the middle of a very bitter war—but the quality of his writing was always considered elegant. Professor Brander Matthews wrote that "he is indisputably one of the loftiest of the lyric poets of Greece, with a surpassing strength of wing for his imaginative flights, and with a surprising sweep of vision when he soars on high."[6] He held a wide variety of interests and passions that were expressed in his writing. He examined politics (*The Knights*, *The Acharnians*, and *Lysistrata*, among others), philosophy (*The Clouds*), and law (*The Wasps*), and in *The Frogs* he embedded a bit of a clinic on literary aesthetics. Eleven intact plays out of a possible thirty written by Aristophanes have survived.

Aristophanes's plays reflect the times he lived in. Athens was a growing power, but perched on the precipice of a great collapse resulting from a prolonged war with rival city state, Sparta. His plays decry corruption and greed, and condemn war—if not all war, at least the particular war

---

4   Qtd. in Bernard Freydberg, *Philosophy and Comedy: Aristophanes, Logos, and Eros* (Bloomington: Indiana UP, 2008), 4.

5   "Possibly," "probably," and "it's likely" are all terms that are widely employed when discussing the lives of the ancient playwrights. In our modern world—a world in which we are familiar with almost everyone, having their biographies instantly chronicled on Facebook, in video, on phones and iPads—it feels odd, but the fact is that biography was a field that was only in its infancy during the Old Comedy period. Writing materials were expensive and storage was always iffy. So facts about the playwrights are few and far between. Many of the "facts" that we receive about playwrights are purely anecdotal and most the results of conjecture of historians piecing together lives hundreds of years after their deaths.

6   Brander Matthews, *The Development of the Drama* (New York: Charles Scribner's Sons, 1912), 80.

that Athens found itself embroiled in. After Athens lost the war, and was occupied by Spartans, the works of Aristophanes—understandably perhaps—adopted a much more subdued tone, and concerned themselves with different subject matter.

QUOTATIONS FROM ARISTOPHANES

"The wise can profit by the lessons of a foe."[7]
—*The Birds*

"For magnificent thoughts we must have magnificent words."[8]
—*The Frogs*

"You will never make the crab walk straight."[9]
—*Peace*

ARISTOPHANES'S EXISTING PLAYS

Akharneis (*The Acharnians*)
Hippeis (*The Knights*)
Nephelai (*The Clouds*)
Sphekes (*The Wasps*)
Eirene (*Peace*)
Ornithes (*The Birds*)
Lysistrate (*Lysistrata*)
Thesmophoriazusae (*The Women Celebrating the Thesmophoria*)
Batrakhoi (*The Frogs*)
Ecclesiazousae (*The Assemblywomen*)
Plutus (*Wealth*)

---

7   Aristophanes, *The Birds* (The Internet Classics Archive). http://classics.mit.edu /Aristophanes/birds.html.

8   Aristophanes, *The Frogs*, in *Aristophanes: Four Comedies*, ed. and trans. William Arrowsmith (Ann Arbor, MI: U of Michigan P, 1994), 68.

9   Aristophanes, *Peace*, in *The Eleven Comedies* (Project Gutenberg, 2005), www.gutenberg.org/cache/epub/8688/pg8688.txt.

MENANDER
342–291 BCE

Menander's representation of every character and of every
grace surpassed all the ingenuity of the old comic poets.
—Dio Chrysostom,
Letter On Oratorical Education[10]

If only a small portion remains of Aristophanes's work, it must be said
that there is even less that has survived of Menander's writings. This is a
great pity considering the tremendous influence Menander had upon the
comic theatre form. What remains with us today represents the only intact
representation of what is known as New Comedy. Until relatively recently
there was almost nothing—mere fragments of scripts and a number of
related quotes—and yet it's believed that Menander wrote something in the
realm of 108 plays. Although eleven of them are known to have existed as
late as the eleventh century, only one intact play survived: *Dyskolos* (*The
Grouch*), rediscovered in Egypt in 1952. Fragments—some of them significant portions—of several other plays were later found, again in Egypt,
among manuscripts that had been used as stuffing for a mummy case.[11]

Born in the latter half of the fourth century BCE, Menander was an
Athenian citizen, raised in a privileged setting, reared by a well-established
family. He had his first play produced while he was still very young, and
his work proved enormously popular in its time and remained popular
long after his death. For example, we know that Menander won first prize
at the festival of Lenaia in Athens eight times, once for his surviving play,
The Grouch.

He wrote during a time of tremendous political upheaval. Athens was
no longer a leading power and was experiencing considerable political
turmoil. Menander's work is a reflection of those times—if it had ever
been "safe" to address political issues, it no longer was. Instead of dealing

10   Qtd. in Orestis Karavas and Jean-Luc Vix, "On the Reception of Menander in
the Imperial Period," in *Menander in Contexts*, ed. Alan H. Sommerstein (New York:
Routledge, 2013), 184.

11   It's worth meditating on a certain paradox here. Menander's manuscripts suffered
the indignity of becoming mere stuffing. But had they not suffered that indignity, they
would never have survived to contemporary times. There's a message of some kind in
there somewhere.

with political matters then, it is romance and personal relationships that drew his attention.

Menander presents a very different face of Greek comedy. His work is less dependent upon issues or ideas than those of Aristophanes, and is more dependent on character. There is less flamboyance to the comedy, less absurd flair or interest in the exotic. He understands that relationships can provide the basis for humour, and so we begin to look at romantic comedy as a staple for the next several hundred years. Nor was it only romantic love he was interested in. It is the love between parents and children, and between siblings.

It is this change to a more subdued, realistic style that results in the quote by Aristophanes of Byzantium (a Greek scholar and critic not related to the playwright), "Oh Menander and Life, which of you copied from the workmanship of the other?" Still, it is worth remembering that it is difficult to extrapolate an overall literary style, based solely on the relatively small sampling that is Menander's work. As Duckworth observes in *The Nature of Roman Comedy*, "We have no assurance that Diphilus, Philemon and other playwrights of the period handled their themes and portrayed their characters in the delicate and refined manner characteristic of Menander."[12]

QUOTATIONS FROM MENANDER

"He whom the Gods love dies young."[13]
—*The Double Deceiver*

"In everything success depends on finding the right time."[14]
—*Dyskolos* (*The Grouch*)

---

12   George E. Duckworth, *The Nature of Roman Comedy*, 2nd ed. (Norman: U of Oklahoma P, 1994), 28.

13   Duckworth, 26.

14   Menander, *Dyskolos*, in *Menander: The Plays and Fragments*, trans. Maurice Balme (Oxford: Oxford UP, 2001), 8.

MENANDER'S EXISTING PLAY

Dyskolos (The Grouch)

Significant fragments from these works have also been published:

Karachedonois (The Man from Carthage)
Kolax (The Flatterer)
Koneiazomenai (The Women Drinking Hemlock)
Leudadia (The Girl from Leukas)
Perinthia (The Girl from Perinthos)
Phasma (The Apparition)
Theophoroumene (The Girl Possessed)

EPICHARMUS OF KOS
540–450 BCE

There is very little known of this ancient poet, philosopher, and comedian, and none of his plays have survived to contemporary times. Commentary hints that this prominent Sicilian is one of the earliest individuals to have written plot-driven comedy, and may have produced comic plays in the era of the earliest Athenians.

As Hugh Denard observes, "Plato, although a contemporary of Aristophanes, has Socrates deem Epicharmus the 'best of comic playwrights.'"[15]

THE GREAT GREEK UNKNOWN

Epicharmus is only one of many. Phormos is also mentioned as being an early playwright who may have been important to the development of comedy. None of his works are with us today. There are many others of whom very little is known. They are mentioned in commentaries, their works are sometimes quoted, and infrequently there are fragments or passages that remain of their works. Included among these forgotten comic

---

15   Hugh Denard, "Lost Theatre and Performance Traditions in Greece and Italy, McDonald," in *The Cambridge Companion to Greek and Roman Theatre*, ed. Marianne McDonald and J. Michael Walton (New York: Cambridge UP, 2007), 144.

playwrights would be Cratinus, Crates, Eupolis, Phrynichus, Philemon, Apollodorus, and many, many others.

As a result of this erasure, it is easy to ignore them, but these writers only escaped posterity as the result of the slightest chance.

THE SATYR PLAYS

The Satyr plays were short tragicomic plays that were presented along with a trilogy of tragic works during the Festival of Greater Dionysia.

As Harry Levin describes these texts, "The Greeks seem to have recognized a third dramatic genre in the satyr play, which seems to have been a sort of mythological burlesque."[16] The Satyr plays first appear around 500 BCE. Some feel that they sprang from dithyrambs (a choral celebration of the god Dionysus that was both sung and danced), but there is no certainty on this matter. Pratinus of Plius is believed to have been the first to introduce this form.

Only one, not particularly comic, intact Satyr play still exists today: Euripides's *Cyclops*, which is based upon Odysseus's encounter with those mythical giants.

16   Harry Levin, *Playboys and Killjoys: An Essay on the Theory and Practice of Comedy* (Toronto: Oxford UP, 1988), 15.

II. THE ROMANS

The Roman Theatre of Catania, in Sicily.

TITUS MACCIUS PLAUTUS
254–184 BCE

In this he [Plautus] was no mere translator, as used to be believed; while still adhering to the main outlines of the original plots and thematic developments, Plautus introduced much original material of specifically Roman flavor, along the way changing everything from the characters' names to the meters used. The stylistic and comic language of Plautus's plays is therefore his, not Menander's, and Latin, not translated Greek.

—Benjamin W. Fortson,
Language and Rhythm in Plautus

The earliest corpus of Latin literature is that of Titus Maccius Plautus, poet and playwright. It's important to note that this first impulse for Latin literature arises out of the Greek theatre. This creates a special type of theatre, the *fabula palliata*, comedies based upon Greek subject matter. But Plautus did much more than translate Greek works, he adapted and transformed them. He dispensed with what remained of the Greek chorus and made the plays more theatrical, more musical, with a good portion being sung. He also created sly references to Rome, and life in Rome, throughout.

It's generally believed that Plautus was born in Sarsina, in Umbria. There is some thought that he was involved in the theatre at an early age. He may have been a scenic carpenter, or, some suggest, an actor. There is the belief that he may have been in the military, and there is folklore that he was involved in commercial interests that went bad, and that he worked for some time milling grain.[17] The story has it that while he milled he translated Greek plays. Of course, none of this information can be confirmed. How he was educated, how he was exposed to the plays of the Greeks, how he became such a talented translator and learned to write such creative Latin nobody knows. Where he gained his thorough knowledge of the theatre, again, is unknown—there is little to go on.

Much of what passes for biographical information is based upon tendencies that appear in his writing. Military terms, symbols, and strategies appear repeatedly in his works, leading some to use this as evidence that he served time in the military. He demonstrates knowledge about matters in the theatre, which can lead to the assumption that he worked as a stage hand or actor. Again, none of this can be proven. We know that his work was immensely popular. He had a great and creative grasp of Latin; this is evident in his writing. His work was exuberant. He had tremendous spirit of invention and appeared to thoroughly enjoy inventing new terms and words. He gloried in writing in a variety of rhythms and tempos.

As E.W. Handley wrote in his comparison of Plautus and Menander, "Plautus likes his colors stronger, his staging more obvious, his comedy more comic."[18] The plays of Plautus were earthy and focused heavily

---

17   Duckworth, 50.

18   E.W. Handley, *Menander and Plautus: A Study in Comparison* (London: University College London, 1968), 18.

upon entertainment. He was considered one of the common people, and he may very well have been, inasmuch as his familial history is unknown.

At one time it was believed that he had written as many as a hundred plays, though that estimate has since been adjusted to thirty or forty. Many plays were credited to him, but a number of these appear to have been counterfeits created by others as a way of attracting attention. In any case, there exist today twenty surviving intact plays.

What strengths does Plautus bring to the craft of writing comedy? He delights in a speedy narrative. His plays are punchy—although they are based upon Greek plays, he has little use for the choral interludes. He keeps his protagonists busy. His intention is to entertain and so he applies multiple strategies—wordplay, an assortment of rhythms, rhyme, staged fighting, cheap jokes. His plays abound with comic asides where characters directly address the audience. And while his works tend towards the crude, rough, and bawdy, there are interesting exceptions. *The Rope* and *The Captives*, for instance, are much more nuanced comedies, and offer rich, layered characterizations.

QUOTATIONS FROM PLAUTUS

"Practice what you preach."[19]
—Asinaria

"Each man must mow his own field."[20]
—Mostellaria

"The mouse never entrusts its life to only one hole."[21]
—Truculentus

---

19   Plautus, *Asinaria*, in *Plautus: The Comedies*, vol. 2, ed. David R. Slavitt and Palmer Bovie (Baltimore: Johns Hopkins UP, 1995), 128.

20   Plautus, *Mostellaria*, in *Plautus: The Comedies*, vol. 2, ed. David R. Slavitt and Palmer Bovie (Baltimore: Johns Hopkins UP, 1995), 368.

21   Plautus, *Truculentus*, ed. Henry Thomas Riley (Persus Digital Library). www.perseus.tufts.edu/hopper/text?doc=Perseus:text:1999.02.0111.

PLAUTUS'S EXISTING PLAYS

Amphitruo (Amphitryon)
Asinaria (The Asses)
Aulularia (The Pot of Gold)
Bacchides (The Two Bacchides)
Captivi (The Captives)
Casina
Cistellaria (The Casket)
Curculio
Epidicus
(Menaechmi) The Brothers Menaechmus
Mercator (The Merchant)
Miles Gloriosus (The Braggart Soldier)
Mostellaria (The Haunted House)
Persa (The Persian)
Poenulus (The Carthaginian)
Pseudolus
Rudens (The Rope)
Stichus
Trinummus (The Three Penny Day)
Truculentus

The Roman Forum, site of the initial performance of *Curculio* by Plautus.

PUBLIUS TERENTIUS AFER (TERENCE)
195/185–159 BCE

Plautus aimed at making the Vulgar laugh; which Aim
he obtained, and not without giving some Pleasure to the
noble, the learned and the wise. Terence was ambitious of
being admired by the judicious few, and he has gained the
Admiration of all who could taste, for near two thousand
years, and not without Wit and Humour, cloathed with
Purity and Delicacy.

—Thomas Cooke,
Terence's Comedies

The last of the famous four ancient comic playwrights, Terence suffers somewhat from his proximity in time to Plautus. As a consequence of this closeness,
he is almost always introduced by way of comparison. Terence arrived on the
theatre scene shortly after Plautus, his body of work is thinner, and it was
not as widely embraced as the work of Plautus. For all that, his plays had
ardent supporters during his career. The material was later enthusiastically
embraced by monks and scribes as some of the finest Latin writing and his
entire corpus of six plays has survived into contemporary times as a result of
this attention. In addition, the innovative approach he took to adapting plays
has made a valuable contribution to comedic literature.

It is claimed that Terence was brought to Rome as a slave, purchased
by Senator Terentius Lucanus. It has been inferred from his name, Afer,
that Terence originated in northern Africa, some suggest Carthage. He
received education (and, one assumes, exposure to Greek plays) in the
household of Senator Lucanus, and was eventually freed. At some point,
the adult Terence began adapting works for the theatre. He was invited
to read one of his plays, *Andria*, to playwright Caecilius Statius, who, it
is said, "He made a good impression on."[22] This began Terence's short
career as a writer, penning a total of six plays, which were presented in
the years 166 through 160 BCE.

---

22   Betty Radice, introduction to *Terence: The Brothers and Other Plays* (New York:
Penguin, 1965), 8.

The works of Terence demonstrate a number of singular strengths. His style of writing is more like natural dialogue. Where the adaptations of Plautus are robust and take great liberty with the language, inventing terms along the way, Terence is renowned for his clear, clean, elegant writing style. Terence completely embraced and refined the parallel stories structure, and began to craft comedy around social issues.

In 160 BCE it's asserted that Terence left Rome on a trip to Greece—perhaps to obtain new scripts to adapt—and died during the voyage. He was still very young at the time, and who knows what he might have contributed or accomplished had he lived on?

QUOTATIONS FROM TERENCE

"Fortune favors the brave."[23]
—*Phormio*

"Time assuages human sorrow."[24]
—*The Self Tormentor*

"I am a man *and* nothing that concerns a man do I deem a matter of indifference to me."[25]
—*The Self Tormentor*

THE PLAYS OF TERENCE

Andria (*The Girl from Andros*)
Adelphoe (*The Brothers*)
Eunuchus (*The Eunuch*)
Hecyra (*The Mother-in-Law*)
Heauton Timorumenos (*The Self Tormentor*)
Phormio

---

23   Terence, *Phormio*, in *Terence: The Brothers and Other Plays*, ed. and trans. Betty Radice (New York: Penguin, 1965), 200.

24   Terence, *The Self Tormentor*, ed. Henry Thomas Riley (Project Gutenberg, 2005). www.gutenberg.org/files/22188/22188-h/files/terence3_4.html#tormentor.

25   Terence, *The Self Tormentor*.

LIVIUS ANDRONICUS
C. 286/260–200 BCE

This Greek slave is credited with being the first poet to write a play in Latin. The details of his life are vague, but it's said he was captured in Tarentum, sold into slavery, and ended up teaching the children of a noble Roman family. While working in the capacity of a tutor he translated several Greek plays into Latin as tools to instruct. He later performed the plays, and though it is said the plays were not especially good, his translations were groundbreaking and proved very influential. They provided the platform for all the subsequent Roman writers of comedy and tragedy. No works of his remain.

GNAEUS NAEVIUS
C. 270–201 BCE

Gnaeus Naevius was one of the more important Roman playwrights of his time. Although he wrote works in a tragic vein as well, he was considered one of the great Roman comedians. (He was also something of an innovator in that he not only adapted Greek works, but he generated original material called *fabula praetexta*, tragic works based on Roman historical events.)

His comedic work included *The Quadruplets*, *The Soothsayer*, *The Lion*, *The Trick*, and *The Potter*.[26] We know of these plays from commentaries, though none of the scripts have survived.

His plays contained critiques of some of the powerful Roman families, which, apparently, landed him in hot water. He was first imprisoned for this libel, then pardoned and released. His writing continued to offend, however, and we are told he was exiled to Utica, where he died.

---

26 Duckworth, 42.

THE GREAT ROMAN UNKNOWN

In the same way that there are many Greek playwrights whose writings have been lost, there were many Romans about whom little can be said because no trace remains of their work, among them: Caecilius Statius, Licineus, Atilius, Turpilius, Trabia, and others.[27]

---

27   Duckworth, 46.

3. CONFLICT, OR PICKING YOUR FIGHTS

The comic plays of ancient times were, in one sense, extended poems—they were poetic in their use of language and in the metres they employed. Two things, however, principally separate the comic plays from other comic poetic forms, the first being that the comic plays were intended to be performed by actors, and the second being that each play had at its core a dramatic conflict that was advanced through action.

The ancient comedians were adept at first selecting those particular moments when conflict was ripe to explode and then tracking that engagement through the escalating staircase of colliding events. So, when the play *Lysistrata* by Aristophanes opens, the Athens/Spartan conflict has already placed the women of Greece in an unbearable situation. The men of the two warring city states are absent from their homes, many dying in battle. The Greek countryside is ravaged by fire and beset by skirmishing soldiers. Lysistrata, the protagonist of the play, believes that the time has come for the women of Athens and Sparta to intervene and take an active part in ending the war. She convenes her female colleagues from Athens, Sparta, and Corinth and challenges them.

LAMPITO
Well then, tell us what you want of us.

CLEONICE
Yes, please tell us! What is this very important business you wish to inform us about?

LYSISTRATA
I will tell you. But first answer me one question.

CLEONICE
Anything you wish.

LYSISTRATA
Don't you feel sad and sorry because the fathers of your children are far away from you with the army? For I'll wager there is not one of you whose husband is not abroad at this moment.

CLEONICE
Mine has been the last five months in Thrace—looking after Eucrates.

MYRRHINE
It's seven long months since mine left for Pylos.

LAMPITO
As for mine, if he ever does return from service, he's no sooner home than he takes down his shield again and flies back to the wars.

LYSISTRATA
And not so much as the shadow of a lover! Since the day the Milesians betrayed us, I have never once seen an eight-inch gadget even, to be a leathern consolation to us poor widows... Now tell me, if I have discovered a means of ending the war, will you all second me?

CLEONICE
Yes verily, by all the goddesses, I swear I will, though I have to put my gown in pawn, and drink the money the same day.

MYRRHINE
And so will I, though I must be split in two like a flat-fish, and have half myself removed.

LAMPITO
And I too; why to secure peace, I would climb to the top
of Mount Taygetus.

LYSISTRATA
Then I will out with it at last, my mighty secret! Oh! sister
women, if we would compel our husbands to make peace,
we must refrain...

CLEONICE
Refrain from what? tell us, tell us!

LYSISTRATA
But will you do it?

MYRRHINE
We will, we will, though we should die of it.

LYSISTRATA
We must refrain from the male altogether...[1]

In a few short strokes the essential conflict is introduced. Lysistrata
insists that the war is intolerable and proposes that if the fighting is to be
stopped, the women must uniformly deny their men any sexual favours
until a truce has been signed by representatives of the warring cities.
With this challenge revealed and the lines of conflict clearly drawn, the
play advances.

In *The Pot of Gold*, Plautus presents Euclio, a miserly figure already in
serious conflict with his household and society around him. He is a man
obsessed with safeguarding a pot of gold he possesses, and he is absolutely
certain that someone will discover where he has hidden it and attempt to
steal it. Plautus seizes a moment when this intolerable, untenable obsession
must be resolved. Euclio explodes onto the stage immediately after the

---

1   Aristophanes, *Lysistrata*, trans. Anonymous (U of Adelaide). https://ebooks
.adelaide.edu.au/a/aristophanes/lysistra/.

prologue, beating his servant as he tries to keep her from discovering—or inadvertently revealing—his secret:

> EUCLIO
> Out, I tell you, out! You have to be outside,
> You prying snoop, with eyes popping out of your head.
>
> STAPHYLA
> Why beat me? I'm bad enough off.
>
> EUCLIO
> To keep you well off,
> And let a bad thing get the worst it deserves.
>
> STAPHYLA
> But why did you shove me out of the house just now?
>
> EUCLIO
> You want reasons from me, you bundle of bruises?
> Move over there, away from the door. Just look
> At her creep. Would you like to know what you're in for?
> Let me lay my hands on a club or a slat, and I'll raise
> The beat of that tortoise pace.[2]

From the moment the play opens, we are introduced to a man whose obsession is clearly out of control. The miserly Euclio is already wound up very tightly, and he is further tested when his wealthy neighbour, Megadorus, approaches him to arrange a marriage with Euclio's daughter. This, Euclio feels, can only bring too many others into close proximity with his precious pot of gold!

It is conflict that offers the key to unlocking character: conflict with the men of Athens reveals the liberating genius of Lysistrata; conflict exposes and lances the stifling obsession of Euclio and fuels his anarchic miserly energy.

---

2   Plautus, *The Pot of Gold* in *Plautus: The Comedies*, vol. 2, ed. David R. Slavitt and Palmer Bovie, trans. Palmer Bovie (Baltimore: Johns Hopkins UP, 1995), 98.

In a sense, conflict creates a special arena, the boundaries drawn by opposing desires, in which character is exposed in a unique fashion. It permits the audience to observe characters making choices under pressure, and consequently it allows the audience to understand the characters beyond the usual polite, careful, safe veneer of societal convention. Whether it is Aristophanes, Menander, Plautus, or Terence, we see the comic playwrights selecting dynamic points of entry into narratives that are ripe with potential conflict.

4. A WORLD TURNED UPSIDE DOWN—THE REMARKABLE PROPERTIES OF THE FORBIDDEN, UNEXPECTED, AND INAPPROPRIATE

The comedians of ancient times are justifiably recognized for storylines that are fantastic, flamboyant, and arresting. What is clear in examining these stories is that they begin from fresh and stimulating points of departure.

These points of departure may be characterized as:

I. THE UNEXPECTED

In a sense, every good story contains unexpected moments. If an audience can anticipate the outcome of a story, moment by moment, with any regularity, there is little reason for remaining attentive. The audience will already have successfully predicted the ending and arrived at their own conclusion—they will have, in a sense, already written it for themselves. The comedians of Greece and Rome understood this notion, and so eschewed the conventional or predictable. For instance, it's entirely unexceptional for individuals to take a cynical view of society and wish for a better way of life. It's *unconventional* to approach birds to solicit refuge. Which, of course, is exactly what Aristophanes has his characters Pisthetaerus and Euelpides do in *The Birds*.

Or, as another example, for as long as there has been war and people have suffered from its depredations, people have longed for the individual power to bring war to a peaceful conclusion. That's expected. It's entirely *unexpected*, and *unconventional*, when someone climbs onto the back of a giant dung beetle and flies up into the heavens to meet with the gods and appeal for peace. Which is precisely what Aristophanes has his protagonist, Trygaeus, do in the play *Peace*. The play begins with the servants of Trygaeus digging up dung, kneading it into a kind of cake, and then feeding an animal this grotesque product.

SECOND SERVANT
As for me, I will explain the matter to you all, children, youths, grownups and old men, aye, even to the decrepit dotards. My master is mad, not as you are, but with another sort of madness, quite a new kind. The livelong day he looks open-mouthed towards heaven and never stops addressing Zeus. "Ah! Zeus," he cries, "what are thy intentions? Lay aside thy broom; do not sweep Greece away!" Ah! Hush, hush! I think I hear his voice!

TRYGAEUS
(from within) Oh! Zeus, what art thou going to do for our people? Dost thou not see this, that our cities will soon be but empty husks?

SECOND SERVANT
As I told you, that is his form of madness. There you have a sample of his follies. When his trouble first began to seize him, he said to himself, "By what means could I go straight to Zeus? Then he made himself very slender little ladders and so clambered up towards heaven; but he soon came hurtling down again and broke his head. Yesterday, to our misfortune, he went out and brought us back this thoroughbred, but from where I know not, this great beetle, whose groom he has forced me to become. He himself caresses it as though it were a horse, saying, "Oh! my little Pegasus, my noble aerial steed, may your wings soon bear me straight to!" But what is my master doing? I must stoop down to look through this hole. Oh! great gods! Here! neighbours, run here quick! Here is my master flying off mounted on his beetle as if on horseback.[1]

---

1   Aristophanes, *Peace* (Project Gutenberg, 2008). www.gutenberg.org/files/2571 /2571-h/2571-h.htm.

The essential thrust of the play, then, can be said to be based upon an unexpected, extraordinary decision, and it is exactly this astonishing impulse that catches the audience off guard. The entire notion rushes at one in so unanticipated a fashion that it provokes the audience to consider the premise—is it possible/desirable to end war—from a fresh point of view without any previously held reservations or objections.

If the thesis of the play is unexpected, so often is the antithesis. Consider the play *Casina* by Plautus. An Athenian wife, Cleostrata, discovers that her husband, Lysidamus, is planning to have one of his servants marry a young girl, Casina, with whom he then intends to covertly have sexual relations. Cleostrata's response is neither of the more conventional options of I will leave him or I'll confront him. Instead she directs her male servant, Chalinus, to dress up as Casina and replace her at the scheduled tryst, as part of an elaborate ruse to punish and humiliate her husband.

In *The Frogs*, Aristophanes first has Dionysus decide on the unusual course of action of remedying Athens by descending into Hades to fetch back a poet to inspire Athenians. He elects to bring back the esteemed playwright Euripides. When he arrives in Hades, however, there is an additional unexpected turn of events when Dionysus discovers that Euripides is in a contest with the equally esteemed playwright Aeschylus to determine who will sit in the seat of honour next to Pluto. This results in testing their styles of writing.

The audience, captured by these startling proposals, has no time to prepare. Instead it engages in the story moment by moment, attentive to the next astonishing turn of events. There's rare power in applying the unexpected.

II. THE FORBIDDEN

Much of comedy springs from a contrarian impulse—it provides the world with what isn't permitted and therefore can't anticipate. There are ample examples of this contrary, contradictory inclination in ancient Roman and Greek comedy.

Consider some of the most comical moments in ancient theatre and you will detect an act that, if not explicitly forbidden, is at least normally discouraged. One of the most notorious examples drawn from the canon of Greek comedy would include the god Dionysus performing in a shamelessly cowardly fashion as he and his servant descend into Hades, in Aristophanes's play *The Frogs*. Gods, who are deathless and powerful, are normally expected, at the very least, to remain stoic under pressure.

At the conclusion of *Pseudolus*, the nervy eponymous slave returns home in a state of high inebriation, confronts his master, and actually belches in his master's face! This is not only bad form for a slave, but could be expected to have resulted in punishment or death.

Women disguising themselves as men, as they do in *The Assemblywomen*, and then using that disguise to first vote at the Assembly, which women were forbidden from doing by law, and then passing a law that permits them to seize political power is a clear example of acting on illicit impulses. The following scene demonstrates these women embarking on this explicitly forbidden activity:

FIRST WOMAN
As agreed, I have let the hair under my armpits grow thicker than a bush; furthermore, whilst my husband was at the Assembly, I rubbed myself from head to foot with oil and then stood the whole day long in the sun.

SECOND WOMAN
So did I. I began by throwing away my razor, so that I might get quite hairy, and no longer resemble a woman.

PRAXAGORA
Have you the beards that we had all to get ourselves for the Assembly?

FIRST WOMAN
Yea, by Hecate! Is this not a fine one?

SECOND WOMAN
Aye, much finer than the one Epicrates has.

PRAXAGORA
(to the other women) And you?

FIRST WOMAN
Yes, yes; look, they all nod assent.

PRAXAGORA
I see you have got all the rest too, Spartan shoes, staffs and men's cloaks, as it was arranged.

FIRST WOMAN
I have brought Lamias' club, which I stole from him while he slept.

SECOND WOMAN
What, the club that makes him fart with its weight?

PRAXAGORA
By Zeus the Deliverer, if he had the skin of Argus, he would know better than any other how to shepherd the popular herd. But come, let us finish what has yet to be done, while the stars are still shining; the Assembly, at which we mean to be present, will open at dawn.

FIRST WOMAN
Good; you must take up your place at the foot of the platform and facing the Prytanes.

SECOND WOMAN
I have brought this with me to card during the Assembly.

She shows some wool.

PRAXAGORA
During the Assembly, wretched woman?

SECOND WOMAN
Surely, by Artemis! shall I hear any less well if I am doing a bit of carding? My little ones are all but naked.

PRAXAGORA
Think of her wanting to card! ...Let us fix these beards on
our chins, so that they spread all over our bosoms. How
can we fail to be mistaken for men?[2]

With their beards and costumes firmly in place, the women proceed
to the Assembly, where they fool the men, and successfully seize political
power.

In tragic works, individuals tend to behave in the way that their station
in life demands. Where they deviate, they suffer and are punished. In the
play *Hippolytus*, Phaedra lusts after her stepson, and ultimately dies as
atonement for this impropriety. In the play *Agamemnon*, Clytemnestra,
the wife of King Agamemnon, is enraged at her husband's infidelity and
his sacrifice of their daughter so elects to murder him when he returns
home from the Trojan War. She too pays with her life. Not so in comedy.
In *The Assemblywomen*, the women transgress but are rewarded for their
misbehaviour.

The situations encountered in comedy can be as potentially dangerous
as those encountered in tragedy. It's possible that comedy thrives precisely
because the pain in humour is mitigated. The audience can fully engage
with the story without fearing that they will empathically experience
anguish and suffering. Therefore, questions that cannot be examined
in tragedy, because they would be too awful, embarrassing, obscene, or
traumatic, are permitted in comedy, as the outcome would not be crippling. In comedy, individuals regularly transgress, and though they may
be rebuked, and are frequently corrected, they survive.

---

2   Aristophanes, *Ecclesiazusae*, ed. and trans. Eugene O'Neill (Perseus Digital Library).
www.perseus.tufts.edu/hopper/text?doc=urn:cts:greekLit:tlg0019.tlg010.perseus-eng1.

III. INAPPROPRIATENESS OF RESPONSE,
OR DOING IT WRONG

The audience can have their attention caught if the approach selected by a character seems completely inappropriate or wrong. A response may be viewed as "wrong" for a number of reasons: it may be more extreme than required, too illogical, too coarse, too candid, or too obvious.

One of the most striking examples of "doing it wrong" is that of Pseudolus in the play of the same name, when Pseudolus the slave warns his master that he is going to swindle him out of a sum of money before proceeding to do just that.

> CALLIPHO
> There are some things about which we wish to inquire of you, which we ourselves know and have heard of as though through a cloud of mist.
>
> SIMO
> He'll manage you now with his speeches, so that you shall think it isn't Pseudolus but Socrates that's talking to you. What do you say?
>
> PSEUDOLUS
> For a long time you have held me in contempt, I know. I see that you have but little confidence in me. You wish me to be a villain; still, I will be of strict honesty.
>
> SIMO
> Take care, please, and make the recesses of your ears free, Pseudolus, that my words may be enabled to enter where I desire.
>
> PSEUDOLUS
> Come, say anything you please, although I am angry at you.

SIMO
What, you, a slave, angry at me your master?

PSEUDOLUS
And does that seem wonderful to you?

SIMO
Why, by my troth, according to what you say, I must be on my guard against you in your anger, and you are thinking of beating me in no other way than I am wont to beat yourself. What do you think? *(to CALLIPHO)*

CALLIPHO
I' faith, I think that he's angry with good reason, since you have so little confidence in him.

SIMO
I'll leave him alone then. Let him be angry: I'll take care that he shall do me no harm. But what do you say? What as to that which I was asking you?

PSEUDOLUS
If you want anything, ask me. What I know, do you consider given you as a response at Delphi.

SIMO
Give your attention then, and take care and please mind your promise. What do you say? Do you know that my son is in love with a certain music-girl?

PSEUDOLUS
Yea, verily.

SIMO
Whom he is trying to make free?

PSEUDOLUS
Yea, verily and indeed.

SIMO
And you are scheming by cajolery and by cunning tricks
to get twenty minæ in ready money out of me?

PSEUDOLUS
I, get them out of you?

SIMO
Just so; to give them to my son, with which to liberate his
mistress. Do you confess it? Speak out.

PSEUDOLUS
Yea, verily; yea, verily.

SIMO
He confesses it. Didn't I tell you so just now, Callipho?

CALLIPHO
So I remember.

SIMO
Why, directly you knew of these things, were they kept
concealed from me? Why wasn't I made acquainted
with them?

PSEUDOLUS
I'll tell you: because I was unwilling that a bad custom
should originate in me, for a servant to accuse his master
before his master.

SIMO
Wouldn't you order this fellow to be dragged head first to
the treadmills?

CALLIPHO
Has he done anything amiss, Simo?

SIMO
Yes, very much so.

PSEUDOLUS
(to CALLIPHO) Be quiet, I quite well understand my
own affairs, Callipho. Is this a fault? Now then, give your
attention to the reason why I you kept [sic] ignorant of
this amour. I knew that the treadmill was close at hand,
if I told you.

SIMO
And didn't you know, as well, that the treadmill would be
close at hand when you kept silent on it?

PSEUDOLUS
I did know it.

SIMO
Why wasn't it told me?

PSEUDOLUS
The one evil was close at hand, the other at a greater distance; the one was at the moment, the other was a few
days off.

SIMO
What will you be doing now? For assuredly the money
cannot be got in this quarter out of me, who have especially detected it. I shall forthwith give notice to all that
no one is to trust him the money.

PSEUDOLUS
I' faith, I'll never go begging to any person, so long, at all events, as you shall be alive; troth, you shall find me the money; and as for me, I shall take it from you.

SIMO
You, take it from me?

PSEUDOLUS
Undoubtedly.

SIMO
Troth, now, knock out my eye, if I do find it.

PSEUDOLUS
You shall provide it. I warn you then to be on your guard against me.

SIMO
By my troth, I know this for sure; if you do take it away, you will have done a wonderful and a great exploit.

PSEUDOLUS
I will do it, however.

SIMO
But if you don't carry it off?

PSEUDOLUS
Then flog me with rods. But what if I do carry it off?

SIMO
I give you Jupiter as your witness, that you shall pass your life free from punishment.

PSEUDOLUS
Take care and remember that.

SIMO
Could I possibly be unable to be on my guard, who am forewarned?

PSEUDOLUS
I forewarn you to be on your guard. I say you must be on your guard, I tell you. Keep watch. Look, now, with those same hands will you this day give me the money.[3]

Pseudolus, who has been asked to raise funds for his master's son, first warns his master, Simo, that he intends to trick him into releasing the necessary funds, and then, to add insult to injury, bets Simo that even though he has been warned he will be unable to stop him. If you are wishing to fleece someone, warning them beforehand seems terribly misguided.

That Pseudolus advances in such a seemingly improbable, misguided fashion, presents him—and the audience—with an exciting challenge. The warning raises what appears to be an insurmountable obstacle. The bet raises the stakes. That Pseudolus proves he is able to overcome this and other obstacles through quick thinking, determination, and on-the-spot invention seems nothing short of miraculous. Thus, the success of the character, and the play.

The three elements—the unexpected, the inappropriate, and the forbidden—provide the comic writers with forceful levers for turning conventional situations on their sides. As with a kaleidoscope, this twisting in turn fashions a particular lens through which the audience may be permitted to view the mundane, the quotidian, and the pedestrian events of the world as something fresh and invigorating.

---

3   Plautus, *Pseudolus*, ed. Henry Thomas Riley (Perseus Digital Library). www.perseus.tufts.edu/hopper/text?doc=urn:cts:latinLit:phi0119.phi016.perseus-eng1.

5. RELENTLESS OVERWHELMING BUSYNESS OF THE PROTAGONIST

All dramatic characters are active. Activity is the defining element of characters in the theatre; it is through their activity that they are distinguished and best understood by the audience. This is as true of tragic figures as it is their comedic brethren. Oedipus strives to discover the truth. Medea struggles to achieve justice/revenge. The audience understands them best—and remembers them most vividly—as a result of their struggles to achieve their goals. In the hands of the ancient comedians, however, something slightly different occurs. To understand that difference, it may be worthwhile to first examine Oedipus from the tragedy *Oedipus Tyrannus* for a moment.

Attempting to do the right thing for the city of Thebes, Oedipus sends Creon to inquire of the Delphic Oracle about what can be done to remedy the plague that has been afflicting his citizens. Learning that the gods demand that a pollution be cleansed, he seeks the criminal who murdered Laius. Learning that there was a survivor and witness of the murderous attack, he sends for the witness to be brought home and calls for a prophet to be consulted. The prophet, Tiresias, arrives soon, and Oedipus questions him...

The pattern here is quite clear—Oedipus receives information and acts upon it. As he receives updated information resulting from previous actions taken, he takes new actions. There is a logical progression that guides him through the narrative. The audience is able to follow this thread—and through tracking it is permitted to compare Oedipus's actions and judge them as either reasonable or not—because the manner in which the narrative advances is logical.

While the information received from messengers and later Tiresias is surprising, even shocking—involving murder and incest as it does—the pattern through which the information is received is entirely cogent. There is a close alignment between cause and effect in the decisions made by Oedipus. This reflects the concept of mimesis—that the action of the theatre should imitate those patterns that are recognizable in life. But in ancient comedy something else occurred, and comedic characterization evolved in a different direction. Why? Comedy, strictly speaking, is not meant to be a representation of an objective reality; it is instead a representation of a *perspective* of reality. The comic writer is attempting to capture that particular moment that evokes a very specific physical response—laughter. The whole point of the endeavour is to capture that tightly focused vision of realty that makes people laugh, and the success of the project hinges entirely upon producing this result.

Perhaps because of this key difference, the protagonist in comedy operates by a different set of rules. The comic character operates at a pace that doesn't necessarily wait for reality to catch up. In other words, ancient comedies keep their protagonists exceptionally busy. This is certainly true of *The Acharnians* by Aristophanes, in which the protagonist takes on not only his own polis, but the entire social structure and the notion of war itself and ends up having to defend himself in the most unexpected of ways from his outraged community.

DIKAEOPOLIS
Now, look here, Gentlemen, this has gone far enough! This brawling and backbiting is simply too much, and I hereby serve notice that I intend to bite back. "Die," you say, do you? Well, it's Death for Death—REPRISALS, Gentlemen! I hold as hostages your most adored, your dearest friends and relatives—the which I now shall flay and disembowel before your horrified gaze.

He turns on his heel and enters his house.

SECOND KORYPHAIOS
Men of Acharnai, neighbors, what could he mean? Do you think he has one of our children penned up inside his house?

FIRST KORYPHAIOS
Impossible!

SECOND KORYPHAIOS
That may be so but where do you suppose he gets his confidence?

> *DIKAEOPOLIS returns and stands before his door. In his left hand is a large scuttle full of charcoal; in his right, a huge carving knife. The CHORUS recoils in horror.*

DIKAEOPOLIS
Very well, Sirs—stone if you must. But a word of warning: One pebble in my direction, and I'll destroy the scuttle and its Defenseless contents.

Any charcoal-lovers present?

> *He raises the knife.*

By God, I'll find out soon enough.

CHORUS
No! No! Not that!
I can't bear to look!
I'll die!
That scuttle's a schoolmate!
A neighbor!
An old and valued family friend!
No, please! I beg you!
I implore you, whatever you do, DON'T!
No!
No!

DIKAEOPOLIS
Gentlemen, your little friends are doomed. Those howls
and pleas are futile—I refuse to listen.

SECOND KORYPHAIOS
Can't you reconsider, Sir?

Does friendship, tried in the furnace, mean nothing at all
to you?

FIRST KORYPHAIOS
Can you see that even a lump of carbon has feelings?[1]

Driven to take desperate measures, Dikaeopolis moves swiftly, gathering up seemingly random materials, and striking an absurd pose. Before the chorus—or the audience—can fully comprehend what has happened, Dikaeopolis has seized and held up a brazier of coal as a hostage. Though this is a completely irrational act, the community is inspired to take pity on the lump of coal. Dikaeopolis swiftly works against impossible odds and, by adopting a highly improbable strategy, succeeds.

This over-tasking of the protagonist is a common element of the Roman Comedy as well. As Duckworth notes in *The Nature of Roman Comedy*, "The most memorable creations are the brilliant servi callidi of Plautus, in spite of temporary setbacks, they are never really at a loss, and usually carry through their outrageous undertakings to an exultant and laughable conclusion."[2]

This level of intense activity is evident in the play *Epidicus*. Plautus presents the slave Epidicus at the very beginning of the play running—and he never has him stop. In fact, when he is not trying to out-manoeuvre someone else, Epidicus is busy arguing with himself. In the following monologue, observe as Epidicus takes *both* sides of an argument with himself:

---

1   Aristophanes, *The Acharnians* in *Aristophanes: Four Comedies*, ed. William Arrowsmith, trans. Douglass Parker (Ann Arbor, MI: U of Michigan P, 1969), 30–31.

2   George E. Duckworth, *The Nature of Roman Comedy*, 2nd ed. (Norman: U of Oklahoma P, 1994), 252.

EPIDICUS

(to himself) He's gone away from here; you are now alone. In what plight this matter is, you now see, Epidicus. Unless you have some resources in your own self, you are done for. Ruination so great is impending over you—unless you support yourself stoutly, you cannot hold up; to such a degree are mountains of misfortune threatening to tumble on you. Neither does any plan just now please me by means of which to find myself disengaged from my entanglement. To my misfortune, by my trickeries I have forced the old man to imagine that he was making purchase of his own daughter; whereas he has bought for his own son a music-girl whom he was fond of, and whom on his departure he commissioned me about. He now, to please his fancy, has brought another one from the army. I've lost my hide, for when the old man finds out that he has been played tricks with, he'll be flaying my back with twigs. But still, do you take all precautions.

He stands still and thinks.

That's of no use! Clearly this head of mine is addled! You are a worthless fellow, Epidicus. *In another tone.* What pleasure have you in being abusive? Because you are for-saking yourself. What am I to do? Do you ask me the question? Why you yourself, in former days, were wont to lend advice to others. Well, well; something must be found out. But why delay to go meet the young man, that I may know how the matter stands? And here he is himself. He is in a grave mood. He's coming with Chæribulus, his year's-mate. I'll step aside here, whence at my leisure I'll follow their discourse.

He steps aside.[3]

---

3   Plautus, *Epidicus*, ed. Henry Thomas Riley (Perseus Digital Library). http://data.perseus.org/citations/urn:cts:latinLit:phi0119.phi009.perseus-eng1:intro.1.

Epidicus manages to advance *both sides of the conflict* even when on his own. When that internal conflict is interrupted by another participant, he promptly adopts another action—spying so that he can obtain still more information. The comic protagonist maintains a relentless forward motion.

In *The Two Bacchides* by Plautus this quotation from the character Chrysalus perhaps captures this sensibility best:

CHRYSALUS

I haven't any use for those Parmenos, those Syruses, that do their masters out of two or three gold pieces. There's nothing more worthless than a servant without brains: he's got to have a precious powerful intellect: whenever a scheme is needed, let him produce it from his own intellect. Not a soul can be worth anything, unless he knows how to be good and bad both... whatever the situation calls for, that he's got to be.[4]

And it is in *Pseudolus* that we best see the comic character as creationist at work—the comic character who speaks of himself as writing a play.

PSEUDOLUS

Since he has gone hence, you are now standing alone, Pseudolus. What are you to do now, after you have so largely promised costly delights to your master's son by your speeches? You, for whom not even one drop of sure counsel is ready, nor yet of silver nor have you where first you must begin your undertaking, nor yet fixed limits for finishing off your web. But just as the poet, when he has taken up his tablets, seeks what nowhere in the world exists, and still finds it, and makes that like truth which really is a fiction; now I'll become a poet.[5]

In other words, he will become the de facto creator of the story!

---

4   Plautus, *The Two Bacchises*, trans. Paul Dixon (Project Gutenberg, 2005). www.gutenberg.org/files/16564/16564-h/16564-h.htm#Bacchides.

5   Plautus, *Pseudolus*, ed. Henry Thomas Riley (Perseus Digital Library). http://data.perseus.org/texts/urn:cts:latinLit:phi0119.phi016.perseus-eng1.

In the comedies of the ancients, the comic character operates on an incredible level of intense activity and often becomes, in a sense, the co-creator as well. These comic protagonists do not only participate in the world, but also shape the material conditions of the world and adjust the fabric of the narrative, foregoing the staid step-by-step measures of cause and effect. This dramatic architecture offers up a tremendous innovation in comic literature.

6. THE UTILITY OF A GOOD VILLAIN

If the protagonists of comedy operate from a different set of rules than their tragic colleagues, the villains of comedy are equally fashioned of different material.

Candour in a villain seems counterintuitive. If there is an aspect that defines a villain, after all, it is their inclination to do wrong, or at least to vigorously oppose the will of the protagonist. An individual who accidentally does wrong is only pathetic. An individual who purposely pursues evil can be defined as a villain. That being the case, villains most often hide their dark intentions or cloak them in more positive light.

Consider the pattern in the play *Antigone* by tragedian Sophocles. Perhaps not a villain in the classic sense, Creon is certainly the antagonist of the story. His response to Teiresias (the same prophet from *Oedipus Tyrannus*, but with a different English spelling), who confronts him, presents a familiar pattern.

TEIRESIAS
How precious, above all wealth, is good counsel.

CREON
As folly, I think, is the worst mischief.

TEIRESIAS
Yet thou art tainted with that distemper.

CREON
I would not answer the seer with a taunt.

TEIRESIAS
But thou dost, in saying that I prophesy falsely.

CREON
Well, the prophet-tribe was ever fond of money.

TEIRESIAS
And the race bred of tyrants loves base gain.

CREON
Knowest thou that thy speech is spoken of thy king?[1]

In the antagonist Creon, we see and recognize exactly what we expect when someone who, having taken wrong actions, is confronted. He responds defensively, and offers a bit of a counterattack.

In Ballio, the outrageous antagonist of the comic play *Pseudolus*, however, we encounter something entirely different. In Ballio we see a character who is truly villainous—in his flamboyant entrance he berates his slaves in the strongest of terms and whips them—and yet demonstrates no desire whatsoever to hide his flaws or mask them with civility. Entirely aware of his flaws, he glories in them. It is precisely this self-awareness and unnatural candour that makes him comic—*and* it is this candour that makes him a challenging opponent. There is humour to be mined from a villain that neither flees nor hides.

When he is first introduced, the colour of his language paints him a villain, and his violent actions complement that language. Further, the audience discovers that Ballio has cheated Calidorus by selling off the individual Calidorus is in love with. Ballio had previously promised to sell the girl to Calidorus so that he could free her.

It's said that this part was the favourite of the famous actor of ancient times, Roscius, and one can understand why—Ballio is completely engaged in his own duplicitous plans. In this scene, Calidorus seeks to purchase the girl he has fallen in love with from Ballio.

---

1   Sophocles, *Antigone* (Greek Texts). www.greektexts.com/library/Sophocles/Antigone/eng/index.html.

CALIDORUS
What? Have you sold my mistress?

BALLIO
Decidedly; for twenty minæ.

CALIDORUS
For twenty minæ?

BALLIO
Or, in other words, for four times five minæ, whichever
you please, to a Macedonian Captain; and I've already got
fifteen of the minæ at home.

CALIDORUS
What is it that I hear of you?

BALLIO
That your mistress has been turned into money.

CALIDORUS
Why did you dare to do so?

BALLIO
'Twas my pleasure; she was my own.

CALIDORUS
Hallo! Pseudolus. Run, fetch me a sword.

PSEUDOLUS
What need is there of a sword?

CALIDORUS
With which to kill this fellow this instant, and then myself.

PSEUDOLUS

But why not kill yourself only rather? For famine will soon be killing him.

CALIDORUS

What do you say, most perjured of men as many as are living upon the earth? Did you not take an oath that you would sell her to no person besides myself?

BALLIO

I confess it.

CALIDORUS

In solemn form, to wit.

BALLIO

Aye, and well considered too.

CALIDORUS

You have proved perjured, you villain.

BALLIO

I sacked the money at home, however. Villain as I am, I am now able to draw upon a stock of silver in my house; whereas you who are so dutiful, and born of that grand family, haven't a single coin.

CALIDORUS

Pseudolus, stand by him on the other side and load this fellow with imprecations.

PSEUDOLUS

Very well. Never would I run to the Prætor with equal speed that I might be made free.

Stands on the other side of BALLIO.

CALIDORUS
Heap on him a multitude of curses.

PSEUDOLUS
Now will I publish you with my rebukes. Thou lackshame!

BALLIO
'Tis the fact.

PSEUDOLUS
Villain!

BALLIO
You say the truth.

PSEUDOLUS
Whipping-post!

BALLIO
Why not?

PSEUDOLUS
Robber of tombs!

BALLIO
No doubt.

PSEUDOLUS
Gallows-bird!

BALLIO
Very well done.

PSEUDOLUS
Cheater of your friends!

BALLIO
That's in my way.

PSEUDOLUS
Parricide!

BALLIO
Proceed, you.

CALIDORUS
Committer of sacrilege!

BALLIO
I own it.

CALIDORUS
Perjurer!

BALLIO
You're telling nothing new.

CALIDORUS
Lawbreaker!

BALLIO
Very much so.

PSEUDOLUS
Pest of youth!

BALLIO
Most severely said.

CALIDORUS
Thief!

BALLIO
Oh! wonderful!

PSEUDOLUS
Vagabond!

BALLIO
Pooh! pooh!

CALIDORUS
Defrauder of the public!

BALLIO
Most decidedly so.

PSEUDOLUS
Cheating scoundrel!

CALIDORUS
Filthy pander!

PSEUDOLUS
Lump of filth!

BALLIO
A capital chorus.

CALIDORUS
You beat your father and mother.

BALLIO
Aye, and killed them, too, rather than find them food; did
I do wrong at all?

PSEUDOLUS
We are pouring our words into a pierced cask: we are
losing our pains.

BALLIO
Would you like to call me anything else besides?[2]

The manner in which Ballio effortlessly deflects the insults and revels in his villainy is refreshingly unconventional and succeeds on the level of keeping the audience attentive. But his lack of shame does more than surprise and arrest—it provides the character Ballio with room to manoeuvre because he is not limited by any usual timidity. This in turn requires that the protagonist work that much harder to defeat him, as the usual corrective instruments of shame and blame find no purchase.

Think of every outrageous comic villain you have encountered in the theatre and you will find a line that snakes its crooked way back to Ballio. Pseudolus is one of Plautus's most vibrant, active, successful protagonists, and it is in no small part due to the strength and forcefulness of this outrageous antagonist, who assists in challenging and consequently defining the hero.

While Ballio is perhaps the most brilliant of the ancient villains, he is by no means the only one to stand out. In *The Knights* by Aristophanes, Paphlagonian focuses the plans of Demosthenes. Here, Demosthenes describes him to the audience:

DEMOSTHENES
I will begin then. We have a very brutal master, a perfect glutton for beans, and most bad-tempered; it's Demos of Pnyx, an intolerable old man and half deaf. The beginning of last month he bought a slave, a Paphlagonian tanner, an errant rogue, the incarnation of calumny. This man of leather knows his old master thoroughly; he plays the fawning cur, flatters, cajoles, wheedles, and dupes him at will with little scraps of leavings, which he allows him to get. "Dear Demos," he will say, "try a single case and you will have done enough; then take your bath, eat, swallow and devour; here are three obols." Then the Paphlagonian filches from one of us what we have prepared and makes

2   Plautus, *Pseudolus*, ed. Henry Thomas Riley (Perseus Digital Library). http://data.perseus.org/texts/urn:cts:latinLit:phi0119.phi016.perseus-eng1.

a present of it to our old man. The other day I had just kneaded a Spartan cake at Pylos, the cunning rogue came behind my back, sneaked it and offered the cake, which was my invention, in his own name. He keeps us at a distance and suffers none but himself to wait upon the master; when Demos is dining, he keeps close to his side with a thong in his hand and puts the orators to flight. He keeps singing oracles to him, so that the old man now thinks of nothing but the Sibyl. Then, when he sees him thoroughly obfuscated, he uses all his cunning and piles up lies and calumnies against the household; then we are scourged and the Paphlagonian runs about among the slaves to demand contributions with threats and gathers them in with both hands. He will say, "You see how I have had Hylas beaten! Either content me or die at once!" We are forced to give, for otherwise the old man tramples on us.[3]

Paphlagonian is a larger-than-life villain who stands in for Cleon, a real-life contemporary politician who Aristophanes found particularly irksome.

In *The Grouch* by Menander, the surly, taciturn Knemon is the larger-than-life antagonist who focuses the protagonist and centres the play. When Pan draws the attention of Knemon's daughter to Sostratos and makes him fall in love, the obstacle is the grouchy father, Knemon, the eponymous antagonist of the play. As Pan describes him in the opening prologue,

PAN
He doesn't greet the crowd of people... "crowd," did I say? This man's lived a fairly long time and hasn't spoken willingly to anyone, hasn't uttered the first word to anyone except me, Pan, his next-door neighbor. He only does this because he's obligated and he regrets it immediately, I'm sure.[4]

---

3   Aristophanes, *The Knights*, ed. Eugene O'Neill (Perseus Digital Library). http://data.perseus.org/texts/urn:cts:greekLit:tlg0019.tlg002.perseus-eng1.

4   Shawn O'Bryhim, *Greek and Roman Comedy: Translations and Interpretations of Four Representative Plays* (Austin: U of Texas P, 2001), 113.

Knemon has no desire to be social—quite to the contrary; he resists every attempt by neighbours to approach him. He won't even converse with strangers but instead chases them off his property, beating them and throwing clods of dirt at them.

Here's what happens when a servant approaches him for a pot, so that a sacrifice can be made at the shrine of Pan.

Enter KNEMON from his house.

KNEMON
You again?!

SIKON
Oh, boy! What's this?

KNEMON
You're provoking me on purpose. Didn't I tell you to stay away from my door? Give me a strap, old woman!

KNEMON grabs SIKON.

SIKON
No way! Let go!

KNEMON
Let go?

SIKON
Yes sir, by the gods!

KNEMON
Come back!

KNEMON hits SIKON.

SIKON
May Poseidon...

KNEMON
Are you still blabbering?

SIKON
I came to ask you for a pot.

KNEMON
I don't have a pot or an ax or salt or vinegar or anything else. I already told everybody in the neighborhood to stay away from me!

SIKON
You didn't tell me.

KNEMON
Well, I'm telling you now.

SIKON
(aside) Yes, and you're going to be sorry! *(to Knemon)* Tell me, couldn't you say where a person could go and get one?

KNEMON
Didn't I tell you? Are you still blabbering to me?

SIKON
A hearty farewell!

KNEMON
I don't want a "farewell" from any of you.

SIKON
Fare badly, then.

KNEMON
Oh, the incurable evils!

Exit KNEMON into his house.[5]

Knemon, grouch that he is, chases off and pelts whoever comes near, until the very end of the play when at last he is tamed. What makes an unapologetic villain of this kind so useful and rewarding? His or her determined opposition to the protagonist becomes a kind of machine that manufactures plot with every exchange he/she has with the protagonist. In addition, the antagonist articulates and embodies the forces of resistance and consequently allows the audience to understand the human dimension of the forces of antagonism.

This pairing of the prodigiously productive, active, and creative protagonist and the candid, inflexible villain proves especially useful in ancient comic theatre. The characters are more energetically charged than characters in tragedy, and are able to connect with and shape the fabric of the narrative in ways that the characters of tragedy are not.

---

5   O'Bryhim, 126–127.

7. POLITICS, STATUS, HIERARCHY, AND COMEDY

In Old Comedy, it is not uncommon to encounter explicit commentary on the contemporary political situation. Actual political figures are regularly lampooned both directly and indirectly, and actual political issues are addressed, directly and indirectly. This is a fascinating development because, of course, it was dangerous to oppose power. (Aristophanes was, as we know, brought before the court because of statements he had actors make that were critical of high-ranking government officials.) Why was political commentary one of the first impulses of the comic theatre, and why has it persisted as such a rich genre in modern comedy?

The administration of politics is associated with power—the power to shape society, the power to impose certain programs, to advance certain individuals, the power to change, reform, and lead. Comedy represents a singular mechanism through which political power and political privilege may be indirectly challenged, and receive correction. Comedy can be viewed as a relatively non-threatening way of challenging might. On occasion, it may be the only way that the prevailing power may be criticized. Nevertheless, it should be noted that as democracy faded and dictatorships and oligarchies flourished and vied with one another in ancient Athens, one sees that political comedy declined.[1]

The Acharnians, an early play by Aristophanes, is unabashedly political. As Douglass Parker puts it in his introduction to the play, "Certainly *The Acharnians* is about Peace, and for Peace. And we may forever wonder at the make-up of citizenry that would not only allow the performance of such a play, in the depths of a life-and-death war, at a public festival [the

---

1   There may be an interesting topic of research to be pursued in tracking exactly how democratic freedom and the performance of political comedy coexist. Totalitarian states generally—although not always successfully—impose silence on comics. The more a democracy lapses into totalitarianism, the less political comedy is tolerated.

Lenaia] but would also award it first prize in the comic competition."[2] This play rails against a war that was declared between the city states Athens and Sparta. It sets the first scene in a quintessentially political context, at the Pnyx, the meeting place of the Athenian legislature where voting took place. Dikaeopolis, the protagonist of the play, has arrived to argue in favour of striking a peace with Sparta.

> **DIKAEOPOLIS**
> It is the day of assembly: all should be here at daybreak, and yet the Pnyx is still deserted. They are gossiping in the marketplace, slipping hither and thither to avoid the ver-milioned rope. The Prytanes even do not come: they will be late, but when they come they will push and fight each other for a seat in the front row. They will never trouble themselves with the question of peace. Oh! Athens! Athens! As for myself, I do not fail to come here before all the rest, and now, find myself alone, I groan, yawn, stretch, break wind, and know not what to do; I make sketches in the dust, pull out my loose hairs, muse, think of my fields, long for peace, curse town life and regret my dear country home, which never told me to "buy fuel, vinegar or oil"; there the word "buy" which cuts me in two, was unknown; I harvested everything at will. Therefore I have come to the assembly fully prepared to bawl, interrupt and abuse the speakers, if they talk of anything but peace.[3]

In this play Dikaeopolis is able to expose the folly of the war, argue on behalf of a negotiated peace, and then physically demonstrate the positive outcomes of a peace as contrasted with the continuing depredations of war.

In comparison to the politically oriented Aristophanes, Plautus is often considered one of the least political writers. His works are instead renowned as bawdy, boisterous romps. And yet, while his play *The Captives* is neither a pamphlet opposing slavery, nor can it be viewed in

2   Douglass Parker, introduction to *The Acharnians*, in *Aristophanes: Four Comedies*, ed. William Arrowsmith (Ann Arbor, MI: U of Michigan P, 1969), 3.

3   Aristophanes, *The Acharnians* (Perseus Digital Library). http://data.perseus.org /texts/urn:cts:greekLit:tlg0019.tlg001.perseus-eng1.

any way as a tract for political action, it does offer a bold observation—
bold for its times certainly. The play presents the case that, but for chance,
anybody could become a slave. This observation, if not explicitly political,
can at least be said to have serious political implications for a nation whose
prosperity depended largely on the free labour of an enormous pool of
captive slaves. The belief in the myth of the slave who was inferior and
so *deserved* enslavement was both convenient for Romans and necessary
to the continued smooth operations of their mines, industries, and farms.

In the following scene, Hegio, a wealthy native of Aetolia, discovers that he has been deceived by a captive slave, Tyndarus. Hegio has
purchased some valuable prisoners of war and intends to use the most
valuable one, Philocrates, to exchange for his son, who is being held as a
prisoner in Elis. Tyndarus has ruined his plans, however. He exchanged
identities with his master, Philocrates. His master, pretending to be the
slave, has been released to return home, to Elis, to negotiate the prisoner
exchange. The real identity of Tyndarus is only revealed later and, when
Hegio comprehends that he has been completely deceived and now has
nothing to exchange for his son but a worthless slave, he is furious. Hegio
confronts Tyndarus, but instead of grovelling or pleading, Tyndarus faces
Hegio down.

HEGIO
(to the SLAVES) Put the manacles on this whipp'd villain.

TYNDARUS
(whilst the SLAVES are fastening him) What's the matter?
What have I done wrong?

HEGIO
Do you ask the question? You weeder and sower of villa-
nies, and in especial their reaper.

TYNDARUS
Ought you not to have ventured to say the harrower first?
For countrymen always harrow before they weed.

HEGIO
Why, with what assurance he stands before me.

TYNDARUS
It's proper for a servant, innocent and guiltless, to be full of confidence, most especially before his master.

HEGIO
(to the SLAVES) Bind this fellow's hands tightly, will you.

TYNDARUS
I am your own—do you command them to be cut off even. But what is the matter on account of which you blame me?

HEGIO
Because me and my fortunes, so far as in you singly lay, by your rascally and knavish stratagems you have rent in pieces, and have distracted my affairs and spoiled all my resources and my plans, in that you've thus robbed me of Philocrates by your devices, I thought that he was the slave, you the free man. So did you say yourselves, and in this way did you change names between you.

TYNDARUS
I confess that all was done so, as you say, and that by a stratagem he has got away from you, through my aid and cleverness; and prithee, now, do you blame me for that, i' faith?

HEGIO
Why, it has been done with your extreme torture for the consequence.

TYNDARUS
So I don't die by reason of my misdeeds, I care but little. If I do die here, then he returns not, as he said he would; but when I'm dead, this act will be remembered to my honor,

that I caused my captive master to return from slavery and the foe, a free man, to his father in his native land; and that I preferred rather to expose my own life to peril, than that he should be undone.

HEGIO

Take care, then, to enjoy that fame at Acheron.

TYNDARUS

He who dies for virtue's sake, still does not perish.

HEGIO

When I've tortured you in the most severe manner, and for your schemes put you to death, let them say either that you have perished or that you have died; so long as you do die, I don't think it matters if they say you live.[4]

As the slave Tyndarus bravely maintains that the deception has been performed for virtue's sake, there can be no question that he demonstrates the nobler character than the free citizen, Hegio, nor can it be questioned that Plautus *intends* him to be viewed that way by the audience.

As comedies go, *The Captives* is a dark one. Tyndarus is threatened with and receives some of the most extreme punishment possible. It's important to note that Plautus continues to remind the audience that this play is indeed a comedy, and maintains the essential tenor of the piece by planting some sassy comebacks in the mouth of Tyndarus.

Plautus also makes some very telling observations about class in the play *The Pot of Gold*. In it, miserly Euclio addresses his concerns about "mixing" classes to Megadorus, his wealthier neighbour.

EUCLIO

Here's what comes to my mind, Megadorus:
You are wealthy and a man of influence,
But I am poor, the poorest of the poor.

---

4   Plautus, *Captivi: The Captives*, trans. Henry Thomas Riley (Perseus Digital Library). http://www.perseus.tufts.edu/hopper/text?doc=Perseus:text:1999.02.0096.

If I married my daughter off to you,
It seems to me that you would be the ox
And I the donkey. What if I was teamed with you
And couldn't pull my fair share of the load,
I the donkey, would flop down in the mud
And you, the ox, would pay no more attention
To me than if I never had been born.
I'd find you quite unfair, and my own class
Of asses would laugh at me. Then, if it came
To a parting of the ways, I'd have no stable
Place to stand with either of the two groups.
The donkeys would sink their teeth into me,
The oxen would run me through with their horns.
It's very dangerous, this climbing up
From the donkey class into the oxen class.[5]

There is hardly a play in the Greek and Roman comic lexicon that does not feature comedy of hierarchy and exchanges of status because slaves played such a pivotal role in so many ways, in society and on stage.

Certainly there were elements of this kind of comedy of reversal apparent in the work of Aristophanes as well. In *The Frogs*, for instance, the god Dionysus is accompanied by his slave, Xanthias, into Hades, and at every step of the journey the slave is proven to be the more capable, intelligent, honest, and courageous of the two. The slave and master struggle throughout the play, striving to get the upper hand.

In the following passage, Dionysus, disguised as Hercules, and Xanthias have entered Hades in their mission to fetch back a poet from the dead who will then reinvigorate Athens. Aeacus, one of the three judges of Hades, encounters Dionysus and mistakes him for Hercules. Aeacus remembers that Hercules stole Cerberus, the celebrated three-headed watchdog, and, angered, goes away to fetch help to punish Hercules/Dionysus. Dionysus, frightened at the possibility of violence, forces Xanthias to take on the robe of Hercules. Immediately upon exchanging costumes, however, Persephone's attractive maid appears and, thinking that Xanthias is

5   Plautus, *The Pot of Gold*, in *Plautus: The Comedies*, vol. 2, ed. David R. Slavitt and Palmer Bovie, trans. Palmer Bovie (Baltimore: Johns Hopkins UP, 1995), 109.

Hercules, flirts with him and invites him to a feast. Xanthias is happy to oblige, but Dionysus, instantly regretting that he will miss out on the revelry, holds him back and insists that they exchange costumes once more. Reluctantly, Xanthias gives up his lion's robe and club. Dionysus sets out for the feast, but no sooner have they started out when the hostess arrives and accuses Hercules of having stolen food when he was last in Hades. She then turns to summon help to punish him. Dionysus immediately compels Xanthias to exchange roles once more. Aeacus returns at this point to punish Hercules, but Xanthias cleverly turns the costume he's wearing to his advantage.

AEACUS
Seize the dog-stealer, bind him, pinion him,
Drag him to justice.

DIONYSUS
Somebody's going to catch it.

XANTHIAS
(striking out) Hands off! away! stand back!

AEACUS
Eh? You're for fighting.
Ho! Ditylas, Sceblyas, and Pardocas,
Come hither, quick; fight me this sturdy knave.

DIONYSUS
Now isn't it a shame the man should strike,
and he a thief besides?

AEACUS
A monstrous shame!

DIONYSUS
A regular burning shame!

XANTHIAS
By the Lord Zeus,
If ever I was here before, if ever
I stole one hair's-worth from you, let me die!
And now I'll make you a right noble offer,
Arrest my lad: torture him as you will,
And if you find I'm guilty, take and kill me.

AEACUS
Torture him, how?

XANTHIAS
In any mode you please.
Pile bricks upon him: stuff his nose with acid:
Flay, rack him, hoist him; flog him with a scourge
Of prickly bristles: only not with this,
A soft-leaved onion, or a tender leek.

AEACUS
A fair proposal. If I strike too hard
And maim the boy, I'll make you compensation.

XANTHIAS
I shan't require it. Take him out and flog him.

AEACUS
Nay, but I'll do it here before your eyes.
Now then, put down the traps, and mind you speak
The truth, young fellow.

DIONYSUS
(in agony) Man' don't torture me!
I am a god. You'll blame yourself hereafter
If you touch me.

AEACUS
Hillo! What's that you are saying?

THE ANCIENT COMEDIANS   67

DIONYSUS
I say I'm Bacchus, son of Zeus, a god,
And he's the slave.

AEACUS
You hear him?

XANTHIAS
Hear him? Yes.
All the more reason you should flog him well.
For if he is a god, he won't perceive it.

DIONYSUS
Well, but you say that you're a god yourself.
So why not you be flogged as well as I?

XANTHIAS
A fair proposal. And be this the test,
Whichever of us two you first behold
Flinching or crying out—he's not the god.

AEACUS
Upon my word you're quite the gentleman,
You're all for right and justice. Strip then, both.[6]

The joy that Xanthias derives from performing the role of the counterfeit master is only equalled by the pleasure he derives from exposing the cowardice of his genuine master, punishing him and hauling him down from his exalted status. The reversal of status, the counter reversal, and the subsequent jockeying for dominant status is brought to a culmination as both servant and master are whipped and, in a sense, both hoisted by their own petards.

The cultures of Greece and Rome were certainly male dominated, and patriarchal, which by its very definition ensures that there will be

---

6   Aristophanes, *The Frogs* (The Internet Classics Archive). http://classics.mit.edu /Aristophanes/frogs.pl.txt.

unequal distribution of power between men and women. Given that one of comedy's impulses is to explore and upset that distribution of power, it ensures that relations between husbands and wives will be a subject of satire as well. This kind of status competition between the sexes was utilized by the ancient comedians as well. Attend to the pointed directions that are delivered to the "newlywed maiden" regarding the power relations between the sexes in marriage, in this portion of the play *Casina*:

> **TWO MAID-SERVANTS**
> Move on, and raise your feet a little over the threshold, newly-married bride; prosperously commence this journey, that you may always be alive for your husband, that you may be his superior in power, and the conqueror, and that your rule may gain the upper hand. Let your husband find you in clothes; you plunder your husband; by night and day to be tricking your husband, prithee, do remember.[7]

Comedy that satirizes the rich and skewers the powerful treads a delicate line. Comedy that is too overtly political can alienate audiences who wish to escape the trials of the world, who want to be entertained and don't wish to be lectured, and who may not share the same political opinions or views of the writer. The Greek and Roman audiences were not slow to express their displeasure, by voicing catcalls or walking out. In many ways contemporary comedy reflects the same strains that ancient comedy felt. Samuel Goldwyn famously commented, "If you want to send a message, use Western Union."

And yet, there is a hunger in the audience to see power challenged, to see overly proud or incompetent leaders exposed and brought low, to prick egos and expose vanity, and sometimes only comedy is able to do this. Because comedy operates from a distinctly alternative perspective, it can make these dangerous observations without appearing overtly confrontational. It has been said that everything is political, even the personal is political. If that's true, then a comedy that reflects the world and turns it on its head has no option but to be political as well—it can't resist or

---

7   Plautus, *Casina*, ed. Henry Thomas Riley (Perseus Digital Library). http://data.perseus.org/texts/urn:cts:latinLit:phi0119.phi006.perseus-eng1.

escape it, because comedy glories in exchanging roles and bringing the high low; wherever power is situated, so comedy gravitates.

8. ROMANCE AS A CREATIVE CRUCIBLE

It seems that the ancient Greeks didn't have much time for romance. Of the eleven examples we have on hand of Old Comedy, not one turns on a plot involving romance. There is a good deal in the work of Aristophanes about sex and politics, but next to nothing that might be construed as being about romantic attachment.

The earliest comedies are primarily ones dealing with politics.[1] In much of what exists in Old Comedy, the *idea* is what is comic. One can sum up the comic premises very quickly. Women decide to stop the war by withholding sexual favours, or, men flee their obligations and escape to a world ruled by birds, etc.

In New Comedy, however, an entirely fresh impulse takes hold. There can be detected the sense that *character* begins to take precedence over *ideas*, that relationships are vital, and suddenly the social world starts to trump the world of politics. Affairs of the heart take shape and romantic comedy becomes the popular form in comedic theatre for hundreds of years.

In the plays shaped by this new impulse, the characters are generally driven by a powerful desire for *someone*. As the poet Ovid said, "No play of delightful Menander exists without love."[2] The earliest written comic play based upon a love story that is still in existence is *The Grouch*, the sole intact play by the celebrated Menander.

Menander wastes no time establishing the love story and the challenges faced by his infatuated characters. In the prologue to this play, the god Pan explains that there is a girl who lives near a local shrine who has

---

1   At least that is what is surmised from the sampling that exists. It's possible that Aristophanes had a more political inclination than his peers, although the portions of text and the titles that have been found don't appear to indicate this.

2   Qtd. in William Scovil Anderson, *Barbarian Play: Plautus' Roman Comedy* (Toronto: U of Toronto P, 1993), 61.

been raised by a poor, bad-tempered farmer—the grouch of *The Grouch*. Because this innocent girl shows reverence for the nymphs of the shrine, Pan has decided to help her out, despite being the daughter of such an irascible, impious father. Pan has made a rich young man, Sostratos, fall in love with the girl. In this scene Sostratos confesses these sudden feelings to his slave, Chaireas.

CHAIREAS
What's that you say? You saw a freeborn girl
Give garlands to the Nymphs here and you went
Away in love, at once?

SOSTRATOS
At once.

CHAIREAS
That's quick!
Had you decided as you left your home
To fall in love with someone?

SOSTRATOS
Chaireas,
You're laughing at me. I'm in a bad way.

CHAIREAS
I believe you.

SOSTRATOS
That is why I've come with you
To help me, since I think you are my friend
And very competent.[3]

Here we see introduced a device that has since become very common in Romantic comedy—love at first sight. Menander was renowned for his

---

3   Menander, *The Bad Tempered Man*, in *The Plays and Fragments*, trans. Maurice Balme (Oxford: Oxford UP, 2001), 5.

economy and in this brief passage we can see him capturing many elements succinctly. He swiftly establishes the love story and the inherent conflict, and enlists an assistant to help propel the protagonist on his way!

The love story as it came to be understood in New Comedy had remarkable staying power. It became a staple for hundreds of years, and though that most curmudgeonly of historic periods, the Dark Ages, didn't have much use for this genre (or any other dramatic form, for that matter), the love story has, since the Renaissance, come back strong and remained a compelling force.

What gives the love story its enduring popularity? Universality, for one thing. Most people can be expected to experience some kind of feelings of love, infatuation, attachment, or attraction at some point in their life. The stakes are high. If falling in love (or falling out) isn't exactly a life-or-death situation, it can certainly feel that way. In *The Eunuch*, Terence expresses the notion that pursuing love is very much like waging war. As the play begins, a young Athenian man, Phaedria, seeks counsel from his slave, Parmeno. Thais, a courtesan that Phaedria has become infatuated with, has closed her doors to him. Should he, in turn, reject her, Phaedria asks Parmeno. Parmeno suggests that there are strategies that must be followed when one pursues love, and weakness or deviation from a plan can lead to failure and loss.

> **PARMENO**
> I'faith, if indeed you only can, there's nothing better or more spirited; but if you begin, and can not hold out stoutly, and if, when you can not endure it, while no one asks you, peace being not made, you come to her of your own accord, showing that you love her, and can not endure it, you are done for; it's all over with you; you are ruined outright. She'll be jilting you, when she finds you overcome. Do you then, while there's time, again and again reflect upon this, master, that a matter, which in itself admits of neither prudence nor moderation, you are unable to manage with prudence. In love there are all these evils; wrongs, suspicions, enmities reconcilements, war, then peace; if you expect to render these things, naturally uncertain, certain by dint of reason, you wouldn't effect it a

bit the more than if you were to use your endeavors to be
mad with reason.[4]

This passage makes clear how feelings of love can fuel dramatic action.
Erich Segal notes in his book *Roman Laughter: The Comedy of Plautus*
that "the most common dilemma in Plautine comedy is that of the young
man *amans et egens*, 'in love and insolvent' turning to his clever slave for
salvation."[5] The love needn't be pure, or true, or uncomplicated. There
are a number of affairs of the heart that are more affairs of the libido.
What's required is that there is sufficient desire provoked, that action is
needed to fulfill it.

The types of characters that were represented in these love stories,
either acting as obstacles to couples uniting or providing assistance and
aid, were recycled from one romantic comedy to another. So often, in fact,
did these character types reoccur that they were given informal titles: the
young man in love (*adulescens amator*); the irritated, elderly father (*senex
iratus*); the clever slave (*servus callidus*). In New Comedy, a discovery
is made that comic characters can be formed around a specific interior
seed of obsessive desire. This becomes the essence of all the other stock
characters who make an appearance in the comic theatre: the pedant, the
braggart, the glutton, the miser.

As mentioned earlier, the literary critic Henri Bergson wrote that
comedy can result when individuals prove inflexible. Certainly the comedy
of stock characters meets this standard. When characters cannot change
their outlook or actions because of their intense, obsessive desires, comedy
often emerges. So whether it is a miser or a braggart, an infatuated lover
or a lecherous old man, when the powerful desires of characters control
their actions, regardless of the projected opposition or outcome, they
become robotic, as Bergson might have said, and certainly they become
ridiculous—and this results in comedy.

The Blustering Soldier of *Miles Gloriosus* fits this description perfectly.
Pyrgopolinices, a soldierly buffoon who constantly trumpets his military
and sexual accomplishments, makes an extraordinary entrance in the

---

4   Terence, *The Eunuch*, trans. ed. Henry Thomas Riley (Perseus Digital Library).
http://www.perseus.tufts.edu/hopper/text?doc=Perseus:text:1999.02.0114.

5   Erich Segal, *Roman Laughter: The Comedy of Plautus* (New York: Oxford UP,
1987), 15.

play as the triumphant hero returning home and striking an imposing posture—only later having this inflated image punctured by his closest servant. Pyrgopolinices is, in fact, pompous, vain, a braggart, and a coward.

In this scene, as the blustering soldier enters, his servant, Artotrogus, promotes and praises his master, while simultaneously undercutting and diminishing his preposterous claims of military prowess.

PYRGOPOLINICES
Take ye care that the lustre of my shield is more bright than the rays of the sun are wont to be at the time when the sky is clear; that when occasion comes, the battle being joined, 'mid the fierce ranks right opposite it may dazzle the eyesight of the enemy. But, I wish to console this sabre of mine, that it may not lament nor be downcast in spirits, because I have thus long been wearing it keeping holiday, which so longs right dreadfully to make havoc of the enemy. But where is Artotrogus?

ARTOTROGUS
Here he is; he stands close by the hero, valiant and successful, and of princely form. Mars could not dare to style himself a warrior so great, nor compare his prowess with yours.

PYRGOPOLINICES
Him you mean whom I spared on the Gorgonidonian plains, where Bumbomachides Clytomestoridysarchides, the grandson of Neptune, was the chief commander?

ARTOTROGUS
I remember him; him, I suppose, you mean with the golden armour, whose legions you puffed away with your breath just as the wind blows away leaves or the reed-thatched roof.

PYRGOPOLINICES
That, on my troth, was really nothing at all.

ARTOTROGUS

Faith, that really was nothing at all in comparison with
other things I could mention—*(aside)* which you never
did. If any person ever beheld a more perjured fellow than
this, or one more full of vain boasting, faith let him have
me for himself, I'll resign myself for his slave; if 'tis not
the fact that my one mess of olive pottage is eaten up by
me right ravenously.[6]

The fervent desire of Pyrgopolinices to be proclaimed brave, and mil-
itarily and sexually potent, is constantly contradicted by reality and the
perceptions of others, providing the impetus for much comedic action.

Likewise in *The Pot of Gold*, it is Euclio's intense desire to protect
his gold that provides the essential core of his miserly character and the
impulse of the comedy of the play, as can be observed in this scene where
he confronts his servant.

EUCLIO

(to STAPHYLA) Back inside now and look after things.

STAPHYLA

Look after what things in there? Or are you afraid someone will walk off with the house? There's nothing else of
value in our place for thieves. Everything there is full of
emptiness, and draped with cobwebs.

EUCLIO

It's a wonder Jove doesn't turn me into a Philip or a Darius
loaded with ducats, just for your sake, you triple-witch.
And as for those cobwebs, I want them taken care of; they
bring me good luck. I'm poor, I admit it. And I put up
with it. I take what the gods give me. So, back inside, and
lock the door. I'll be back soon. Make sure you don't let
any stranger into the house. Should anyone come around

---

6   Plautus, *Miles Gloriosus*, ed. Henry Thomas Riley (Perseus Digital Library).
www.perseus.tufts.edu/hopper/text?doc=urn:cts:latinLit:phi0119.phi012.perseus-eng1.

looking for coals, I want you to put the fire out, and then no one will have any reason to ask you for a light. If that fire keeps burning, I'll put you out. If anyone asks for water, say it's run out; or an ax, or mortar and pestle, or some cooking pots, things the neighbors are always wanting to borrow: tell them that thieves got in and stole the lot. I don't want a single person let in my house while I'm away, I tell you. And I also tell you: if Good Fortune herself comes along, don't admit her.[7]

This comedy based upon characters possessed by intense desires—be it love, or love of money—conforms to notions of emotional rigidity and exaggeration, of small matters taking on immense significance.

7   Plautus, *The Pot of Gold* in *Plautus: The Comedies*, vol. 2, ed. David R. Slavitt and Palmer Bovie, trans. Palmer Bovie (Baltimore: Johns Hopkins UP, 1995), 100.

9. CONFLICT IN ACTION—
COMEDY AND VIOLENCE

There is an abundance of violence to be found in the works of the ancient comedians. This is perhaps a reflection of the times—which were nothing if not abundantly violent. In Aristophanes's play *Lysistrata*, the chorus of old men, enraged at the temerity of the radicalized women who have occupied the citadel, decide to make a full frontal charge on them. The women respond vigorously. They fight back and the old men are beaten, battered, and thoroughly defeated. In *The Persian*, Toxilus and his comrades give the procurer, Dordalus, a sound drubbing at the conclusion of the play. There is no shortage of this kind of mayhem in the comic plays of ancient Greece and Rome. How, people often ask, can violence possibly be funny?

Certainly in tragedy it's not, nor is it meant to be. The key differences between violence in tragic works and violence in comic works are resilience, scale, and intent. In comedies, violence doesn't result in any lasting suffering. When violence is irreparable, when it is unmediated, when the suffering becomes intense, then it shifts into the realm of the tragic.

In *The Two Bacchides* the clever slave, Chrysalus, attempts to help Mnesilochus, the son of his master, Nicobulus, and in so doing casts himself in harm's way with his master. This scene offers a good example of how the comic treatment of violence differs from that of tragedy.

CHRYSALUS
(solo) What a monstrous concoction of a plot I've got brewing! My only worry is that I may not be able to make the plot work. The first thing I've got to do is get the old man mad and raging at me. It wouldn't be a proper Greek swindle if he saw me in a tranquil, gentle mood. I'll have him turned inside-out today, stake my life on it. I'll roast

him dry as a parched pea. Now to stroll to his door! When he comes out, I'll be placed to put the letter in his hand.

NICOBULUS comes rushing out of his house.

NICOBULUS
What an outrage to my dignity! That Chrysalus has got away from me!

CHRYSALUS
(aside) I'm saved! The old man is angry. Now's the time for me to go up to him.

NICOBULUS
Who is talking over there? Why, I believe it's Chrysalus!

CHRYSALUS
Here it goes.

NICOBULUS
(sarcastically) O excellent slave, greetings. How are things? How soon should I set sail for Ephesus to bring back my gold from Theotimus?

CHRYSALUS does not respond.

Nothing to say? I swear by all the gods that if I didn't love my son so and want to give him anything he asks for, your hide would have been well whipped by now. You could spend the rest of your life in chains at the mill. I've learned all about your crimes from Mnesilochus.

CHRYSALUS
(innocently) He's charged me?

(aside) That's perfect! I'm the one that's wicked and the scoundrel. You just watch what happens! I won't say another word.

NICOBULUS
You cut-throat! Are you making threats?

CHRYSALUS
You'll know soon enough what kind of person he is. He ordered me to bring you this letter. He asked that you do whatever is written here.

NICOBULUS
Hand it over.

CHRYSALUS
Notice the seal.

NICOBULUS
I do. Where is he?

CHRYSALUS
I don't know.

(aside) The only proper things for me is to know nothing. I've forgotten everything

(to NICOBULUS) You know that I'm a slave. I don't even know what I do know.

(aside) Now the little birdie has seen the worm and walked into the trap. With the noose I've set, I'll have this fellow hung up nicely.

NICOBULUS
Just a moment.

Reads the letter.

Aargh! I'll soon come back to you, Chrysalus.

Goes back into his house.

CHRYSALUS
As if he were playing the trick on me! As if I didn't know what he's going to do! He's gone inside to get some slaves to tie me up. But it's his ship of state that's floundering nicely, my little bark is sailing along fine. Now I'll quiet down. I hear the door opening.

Enter NICOBULUS with his slave overseer ARTAMO and other slaves.

NICOBULUS
Now, Artamo, seize that fellow there and tie him up.

ARTAMO and company do.

CHRYSALUS
(feigning innocence) What have I done?

NICOBULUS
(to ARTAMO) Smash him in the face if he lets out a peep!

(to CHRYSALUS) What does this letter say?

CHRYSALUS
Why are you asking me? I took it from him and brought it all sealed to you.

NICOBULUS
Oh, you rascal, you! You've been berating my son because he gave the gold back to me? And you said that you would use some Greek swindle to get the money from me?

CHRYSALUS
(all innocence) I said that?

NICOBULUS
Yes.

CHRYSALUS
Who is it said I said that?

NICOBULUS
Quiet!

   ARTAMO hits CHRYSALUS.

No man said it. The letter you brought here indicts you.

   Points to the letter.

See! These words order you to be tied up.

CHRYSALUS
(takes letter, pretends to read very carefully) Aha! Your
son has made me the courier of my own death warrant, just
like Bellerophon. So, I brought the very letter that orders
me to be tied up? Very well. So what?

NICOBULUS
I'm only doing this to make you persuade my son that he
ought not to live like a degenerate Greek, you wretched
swine.

CHRYSALUS
Oh, you fool, you fool! Here you are, standing on the
block, the slave dealer is calling out your name, and you
don't even know that you're on sale.

NICOBULUS
Tell me, who is selling me?

CHRYSALUS
(to audience) As the poet says,
"He whom the gods love dies young,
while he still has his strength, sense, and wit."

Points to NICOBULUS.

If any god loved this man, he would have died more than
ten years ago—no, more than twenty years ago. This
burden on the earth walks around and knows nothing,
feels nothing. He's as worthless as a rotten mushroom.

NICOBULUS
(to CHRYSALUS) So, I'm a burden on the earth, you say?

(to ARTAMO) Take him inside and string him up tight
to the whipping post. You'll never take my gold away
from me!

CHRYSALUS
Ha! You'll give it away.

NICOBULUS
Give it away?

CHRYSALUS
Yes, and you yourself will beg me to take it away, when
you find out the deadly danger my accuser is in...

(ominously) ...Oh, how much deadly danger. Then you'll
shower liberty all over Chrysalus, but I'll never take it.[8]

8   Plautus, *The Two Bacchides* in *Plautus: The Comedies*, vol. 2, ed. David R. Slavitt
and Palmer Bovie, trans. Palmer Bovie (Baltimore: Johns Hopkins UP, 1995), 215–219.

It is important to recognize a few things in this scene. Though Chrysalus is seized, tied up, and struck in an escalating series of events, and then further threatened with even greater violence, perhaps torture, he maintains his composure and recovers from his manhandling almost instantly. And although Chrysalus is about to be taken away to be tied to a post and flogged, the tone of the exchange remains light, and the blows delivered don't sustain any damage of consequence. There is no intent to alarm the audience, or to imply that Chrysalus will come to any serious, lasting harm. For these reasons, the violence of the scene doesn't distract the audience from the essential intent to amuse.

In *Thesmophoriazusae*, Aristophanes combines pain with indignity as he has the poet Euripides prepare his confederate, Mnesilochus, to attend the festival on his behalf. Mnesilochus must be costumed as a woman, so that he may safely spy upon the women and report back to Euripides what they are saying about him. To successfully accomplish the transformation he must first agree to have his body hair removed—a fairly painful procedure in ancient times.

EURIPIDES
Stand up; I am now going to remove your hair. Bend down.

MNESILOCHUS
Alas! alas! they are going to grill me like a pig.

EURIPIDES
Come now, a torch or a lamp! Bend down and watch out for the tender end of your tool!

MNESILOCHUS
Aye, aye! but I'm afire! oh! oh! Water, water, neighbour, or my perineum will be alight!

EURIPIDES
Keep up your courage!

MNESILOCHUS
Keep my courage, when I'm being burnt up?

EURIPIDES

Come, cease your whining, the worst is over.

MNESILOCHUS

Oh! it's quite black, all burnt down there!

EURIPIDES

Don't worry! Satyrus will wash it.[9]

Once again, while there are howls of pain and exclamations of outrage at the indignity of this procedure, the tone of this scene is comically exaggerated to signal to the audience that the pain is not genuine, and there is no actual long-lasting suffering incurred.

Horror is sometimes expressed by critics of this kind of forceful, physical humour, and concern that an audience too greatly relishes violence, but I believe this speaks to a fundamental misunderstanding of the actual function of violence in comedy. It is the essential indestructability of character that is illuminated by these violent outbursts. Outrage, indignity, blows may all be part of the comic sensibility, but in comedy resilience and recovery are tempering elements that render these events laughable.

In tragic works, individuals tend to behave in the way that their station in life demands. Where they deviate, they suffer and are punished. Already mentioned earlier have been the examples of the play *Hippolytus* by Euripides, in which Phaedra lusts after her stepson, and ultimately dies in atonement for this impropriety; and the play *Agamemnon*, in which Clytemnestra, the wife of King Agamemnon—enraged at her husband's infidelity and his sacrifice of their daughter—elects to murder him when he returns home from the Trojan War, and ultimately pays with her life. There are many other examples. Perhaps one of the most famous illustrations of this exists in *The Bacchae* by Euripides. In it, Pentheus defies the god Dionysus, and as a consequence dies in a particularly gruesome manner—ripped to bits during the Bacchic revelry.

In comedy, characters are able to transgress without suffering terminal sanctions. It is possible that comedy thrives precisely because the pain

---

9   Aristophanes, *Thesmophoriazusae*, ed. Eugene O'Neill Jr. (Perseus Digital Library). www.perseus.tufts.edu/hopper/text?doc=Perseus:text:1999.01.0042.

experienced by the characters is diminished, or at the very least there is the potential for emotional recovery, even though situations can be serious. Questions that cannot be examined in tragedy because they would be too awful, too embarrassing, too obscene, are permitted in comedy because the audience is made to understand that the outcome will not be crippling.

Violence functions as a comic device in the theatre because it is *energetic*, and it provides characters with active strategies to achieve their ambitions. It works because it is a *highly visual device* in what is an essentially visual medium. Characters strike and are in turn stricken, and the audience can see the impact of those blows and judge for themselves how, or whether, the characters have advanced their ambitions. It works primarily because there is *no essential pain felt*—indignity, yes, outrage, yes, but significant pain and suffering, no, and consequently the audience may observe this violence without fear that they will, through feelings of empathy, experience grief and undue suffering themselves.

10. SEXUALITY AND COMEDY
IN THE THEATRE

As part of an article on the meaning of comedy, L.J. Potts wrote, "In its historical beginning comedy was a species of authorized license... What this means is that comedy was a safety-valve or outlet for disorderly passions, including erotic passions, and by treating them in an unserious spirit, it rendered them less dangerous socially."[1]

This is one way of viewing the way sex is explored in comedy, as a kind of "safety valve for disorderly passions"—but if one considers sexuality to be an essential part of existence, then it would be unusual if sex did not receive some kind of comedic attention. Certainly sexual material appears fairly commonly in Greek and Roman comedy, and it manifests itself in a variety of ways. We tend to think that our culture and our times are the most liberal and permissive of eras, that contemporary culture somehow invented sex in the theatre, but that's hardly the case. Among the Greeks and Romans, representations of sexual behaviour in the theatre, most particularly in the comic theatre, were prevalent.

What makes sex so useful to writers of comedy is that the intimacy and passion invested in the exchange endow the activity with high stakes and important symbolic value. After all, sex, while an interesting activity in and of itself, can stand in for so many things. For instance, when Dikaeopolis strokes his naked female partner at the conclusion of *The Acharnians*, it presents an especially graphic metaphor for the triumph of his fertile imagination over the barren martial determination of his fellow citizens. And while it is the fervent yearning and desire for sex that provides Lysistrata with leverage in her peace negotiations with the men of Greece, the happy conclusion portends sexual congress, which

---

1   L.J. Potts, "The Subject Matter of Comedy," in *Comedy, Meaning and Form*, ed. Robert W. Corrigan (San Francisco: Chandler, 1965), 204.

symbolically confirms the men's need for the tempering influence of women.

This play, *Lysistrata*, contains what is, perhaps, the most celebrated scene involving sex in the history of theatre, and it offers tremendous insight into how sexual content was applied by the ancient comedians. In this scene a soldier, Cinesias, attempts to convince his wife, Myrrhine, to abandon her peace protest, return home with him, and enjoy sexual relations. She remains adamant, maintaining that the war must be stopped before she can consummate the sexual act, and she uses Cinesias's sexual longing as inducement in her negotiations with him.

CINESIAS
And Aphrodite, whose mysteries you have not celebrated for so long? Oh! won't you please come back home?

MYRRHINE
No, least, not till a sound treaty puts an end to the war.

CINESIAS
Well, if you wish it so much, why, we'll make it, your treaty.

MYRRHINE
Well and good! When that's done, I will come home. Till then, I am bound by an oath.

CINESIAS
At any rate, lie with me for a little while.

MYRRHINE
No, no, no! *(She hesitates.)* but just the same I can't say I don't love you.

CINESIAS
You love me? Then why refuse to lie with me, my little girl, my sweet Myrrhine?

MYRRHINE
(pretending to be shocked) You must be joking! What, before the child!

CINESIAS
(to the slave) Manes, carry the lad home. There, you see, the child is gone; there's nothing to hinder us; won't you lie down now?

MYRRHINE
But, miserable man, where, where?

CINESIAS
In the cave of Pan; nothing could be better.

MYRRHINE
But how shall I purify myself before going back into the citadel?

CINESIAS
Nothing easier! you can wash at the Clepsydra.

MYRRHINE
But my oath? Do you want me to perjure myself?

CINESIAS
I'll take all responsibility; don't worry.

MYRRHINE
Well, I'll be off, then, and find a bed for us.

CINESIAS
There's no point in that; surely we can lie on the ground.

MYRRHINE
No, no! even though you are bad, I don't like your lying on the bare earth.

She goes back into the Acropolis.

CINESIAS
(enraptured) Ah! how the dear girl loves me!

MYRRHINE
(coming back with a cot) Come, get to bed quick; I am going to undress. But, oh dear, we must get a mattress.

CINESIAS
A mattress? Oh! no, never mind about that!

MYRRHINE
No, by Artemis! lie on the bare sacking? never! That would be squalid.

CINESIAS
Kiss me!

MYRRHINE
Wait a minute!

She leaves him again.

CINESIAS
Good god, hurry up

MYRRHINE
(coming back with a mattress) Here is a mattress. Lie down, I am just going to undress. But you've got no pillow.

CINESIAS
I don't want one either!

MYRRHINE
But I do.

She leaves him again.

CINESIAS
Oh god, oh god, she treats my tool just like Heracles!

MYRRHINE
(coming back with a pillow) There, lift your head, dear!
(wondering what else to tantalize him with; to herself) Is
that all, I wonder?

CINESIAS
(misunderstanding) Surely. There's nothing else. Come,
my treasure.

MYRRHINE
I am just unfastening my girdle. But remember what
you promised me about making peace; mind you keep
your word.

CINESIAS
Yes, yes, upon my life I will.

MYRRHINE
Why, you have no blanket!

CINESIAS
My god, what difference does that make? What I want is
to make love!

MYRRHINE
(going out again) Never fear—directly, directly! I'll be
back in no time.

CINESIAS
The woman will kill me with her blankets!

MYRRHINE
(coming back with a blanket) Now, get yourself up.

CINESIAS
(pointing) I've got this up!

MYRRHINE
Wouldn't you like me to scent you?

CINESIAS
No, by Apollo, no, please don't!

MYRRHINE
Yes, by Aphrodite, but I will, whether you like it or not.

She goes out again.

CINESIAS
God, I wish she'd hurry up and get through with all this!

MYRRHINE
(coming back with a flask of perfume) Hold out your hand; now rub it in.

CINESIAS
Oh! in Apollo's name, I don't much like the smell of it; but perhaps it will improve when it's well rubbed in. It does not somehow smack of the marriage bed!

MYRRHINE
Oh dear! what a scatterbrain I am; if I haven't gone and brought Rhodian perfumes!

CINESIAS
Never mind, dearest, let it go now.

MYRRHINE
You don't really mean that.

She goes.

CINESIAS
Damn the man who invented perfumes!

MYRRHINE
(coming back with another flask) Here, take this bottle.

CINESIAS
I have a better one all ready for you, darling. Come, you provoking creature, to bed with you, and don't bring another thing.

MYRRHINE
Coming, coming; I'm just slipping off my shoes. Dear boy, will you vote for peace?[2]

This scene—this *play*—is, in one sense, entirely about sex; or, rather, it is about the promise of and withholding of sex. Bernard Freydberg maintains that in this case "erōs serves transcendent purposes in *Lysistrata*. The physical beauty and sexual charms of the wives are withheld from their husbands, a withholding that aims at the great political goal of ending warfare, and at the great private goal of familial happiness."[3]

Sexuality when applied to the theatre need not be all about celebration, nor must things conclude happily, however. When, in the play *Casina*, a planned sexual rendezvous is turned into a burlesque fracas, what was to be a consummation is instead transformed into a humbling acknowledgement of defeat. An old and lecherous man, Lysidamus, plots to have sexual relations with Casina, a younger woman servant. He intends for her to marry another of his servants, Olympio, and thus maintain sexual access

2   Aristophanes, *Lysistrata* (U of Adelaide). https://ebooks.adelaide.edu.au/a/aristophanes/lysistra/.

3   Bernard Freydberg, *Philosophy and Comedy: Aristophanes, Logos, and Eros* (Bloomington: Indiana UP, 2008), 174.

to her whenever he wishes—without his wife knowing. It is through the machinations he pursues to achieve this goal and the counter stratagems that his wife advances to prevent this outcome, that the plot of the play is generated. When Lysidamus cannot be deterred in other ways, Cleostrata finally has her servant, Chalinus, disguise himself as the bride, and in this disguise she/he "marries" Olympio.

Olympio and Lysidamus excitedly prepare to enjoy a quick moment of sexual intimacy with the bride in a darkened room over at a neighbour's house following the ceremony. Myrrhina, the neighbour, gloats over what Olympio and Lysidamus will discover.

> **MYRRHINA**
> I'd like to know how Chalinus gets on—the newly-married bride with her new-made husband. Never, upon my faith, any day did I laugh so much, nor in the time that's to come do I think that I shall laugh more; and no poet ever did contrive a more artful plot than this was skillfully contrived by us! I'd now very much like the old fellow to come out, with his face well battered...

And later, when Olympio escapes from the neighbour's house, he is in a state of great alarm.

> **OLYMPIO**
> (to the audience) Lend me your attention, while I repeat my exploits; it's worth your while to catch them with your ears, so ridiculous to be heard, to be repeated, are these mishaps, which I have met with in the house. I had led my new-made bride into the room, I fastened the bolt, but, however, the gloom there was just like the night... When I addressed Casina, "Casina," said I, "my dear wife, why do you slight your husband in this fashion? Really, upon my faith, you do this quite without my deserving it, inasmuch as I have given you preference as my wife." She said not a word. When I attempted a kiss, a beard pricked my lips just like briars. Forthwith, as I was upon my knees,

she struck my head with her feet. I tumbled headlong from
the bed, she leapt down upon me and punched my face.[4]

Shortly after, Lysidamus emerges, equally thrashed and humiliated. His
plan for a sexual assignation, which from the beginning employed sex as
a mechanism of power and control, is turned on its head, as the master
is ultimately mastered. *Casina* permits the audience to translate what
appears to be a failed attempt at covert sex into a sly understanding of
power relations within a family.

In *Casina*, there is a good deal of sexual impropriety that is prevented
from becoming too "real" by the use of cross-dressing and counterfeit-
ing. But it's important to recollect that in the ancient Greek and Roman
theatre, *all* roles were performed by men—including the female roles.
In effect, that meant that there were frequently men wearing masks and
costumes, *pretending* to be women (as in *Casina*), and sometimes these
men pretending to be women were then, in turn, *pretending* to be men, (as
in *The Assemblywomen*). That blurring of lines and boundaries was an
integral part of ancient comedy, and permitted the audience to understand
that however dangerous, challenging, or upsetting the ideas and images
were that were presented, the whole device was an artificial, invented
theatrical construct.

So in the play *Miles Gloriosus*, when Pirip says, "Ah, you've come at
the right moment, Palaestrio. Look! Here they are. The girls you asked
me to bring along, all dressed up,"[5] the audience is taken in on the joke.
"All dressed up" holds a double meaning in this case—and this distancing
permitted the audience to engage in the story without necessarily judging
it on the basis of standard societal conventions.

---

4   Plautus, *Casina*, ed. Henry T. Riley (Perseus Digital Library). www.perseus.tufts
.edu/hopper/text?doc=Perseus:text:1999.02.0097.

5   Plautus, *Miles Gloriosus*, in *Plautus: Three Comedies*, ed. and trans. Peter Smith
(Ithaca, NY: Cornell UP, 1991), 72.

11. VISUAL COMEDY

There is a tendency to think of comedy as something spoken, but it is equally something viewed. The pie in the face is not a verbal laugh, it is a visual laugh. Although Aristophanes is widely touted as a brilliant political comic, less is made of the fact that he is also a brilliant visual comic.

In most of his comedies he made good use of bold visual statements. In *The Acharnians*, an elaborately costumed play within a play is staged to prevent the angry citizens from attacking the protagonist. In *The Birds*, a chorus of men swarm the stage bedecked as a society of birds, and in *The Wasps*, a chorus of men appear out of the darkness dressed as wasps—a visual metaphor for the Athenians' stinging, litigious nature.

LEADER OF THE CHORUS
Why do we delay to let loose that fury, that is so terrible, when our nests are attacked?

CHORUS
(singing) I feel my angry sting is stiffening, that sharp sting, with which we punish our enemies. Come, children, cast your cloaks to the winds, run, shout, tell Cleon what is happening, that he may march against this foe of our city, who deserves death, since he proposes to prevent the trial of lawsuits.

The Boys run off, taking the CHORUS' mantles with them.

BDELYCLEON
(rushing out of the house with the two slaves and seizing his father) Friends, listen to the truth, instead of bawling.

LEADER OF THE CHORUS
By Zeus! we will shout to heaven.

BDELYCLEON
And I shall not let him go.

LEADER OF THE CHORUS
Why, this is intolerable, 'tis manifest tyranny.

CHORUS
(singing) Oh! citizens, oh! Theorus, the enemy of the gods! and all you flatterers, who rule us! come to our aid.

XANTHIAS
By Heracles! they have stings. Do you see them, master?

BDELYCLEON
It was with these weapons that they killed Philippus the son of Gorgias when he was put on trial.

LEADER OF THE CHORUS
And you too shall die. Turn yourselves this way, all, with your stings out for attack and throw yourselves upon him in good and serried order, and swelled up with wrath and rage. Let him learn to know the sort of foes he has dared to irritate.

XANTHIAS
The fight will be fast and furious, by great Zeus! I tremble at the sight of their stings.

CHORUS
(singing) Let this man go, unless you want to envy the tortoise his hard shell.

PHILOCLEON
Come, my dear companions, wasps with relentless hearts, fly against him, animated with your fury. Sting him in the arse, eyes, and fingers.[6]

The genius in costuming the chorus as wasps is that while the image is perfectly comical—one can only imagine what it must have looked like for the chorus of men dressed up as wasps, advancing on the house with their "stingers" presented—the image parallels wasps' actual swarming behaviour with the shrill mob mentality of the unforgiving jury.

In the play *Peace*, Aristophanes employs a stunning visual device to create a dynamic and memorable entrance, as Trygaeus swoops onto the stage on the back of a gigantic dung beetle.

A machine brings in TRYGAEUS astride an enormous figure of a dung beetle with wings spread.

TRYGAEUS
Gently, gently, go easy, beetle; don't start off so proudly, or trust at first too greatly to your powers; wait till you have sweated, till the beating of your wings shall make your limb joints supple. Above all things, don't let off some foul smell. I adjure you; else I would rather have you stay right in the stable.

FIRST SERVANT
Poor master! Is he crazy?

TRYGAEUS
Silence! silence!

---

6   Aristophanes, *The Wasps*, ed. Eugene O'Neill Jr. (Perseus Digital Library). www.perseus.tufts.edu/hopper/text?doc=Perseus:text:1999.01.0044.

FIRST SERVANT
But why start up into the air on chance?

TRYGAEUS
'Tis for the weal of all the Greeks; I am attempting a daring and novel feat.

FIRST SERVANT
But what is your purpose? What useless folly!

TRYGAEUS
No words of ill omen! Give vent to joy and command all men to keep silence, to close down their drains and privies with new tiles and to cork up their own arses.

FIRST SERVANT
No, I shall not be silent, unless you tell me where you are going.

TRYGAEUS
Why, where am I likely to be going across the sky, if it be not to visit Zeus?

FIRST SERVANT
For what purpose?

TRYGAEUS
I want to ask him what he reckons to do for all the Greeks.

FIRST SERVANT
And if he doesn't tell you?

TRYGAEUS
I shall pursue him at law as a traitor who sells Greece to the Medes.

FIRST SERVANT
Death seize me, if I let you go.

TRYGAEUS
It is absolutely necessary.

FIRST SERVANT
(loudly) Alas! alas! dear little girls, your father is deserting you secretly to go to heaven. Ah! poor orphans, entreat him, beseech him.

The little daughters of TRYGAEUS come out.

LITTLE DAUGHTER
(singing) Father! father! what is this I hear? Is it true? What! you would leave me, you would vanish into the sky, you would go to the crows? Impossible![7]

This immensely visual introduction to Trygaeus is surprising, arresting, and represents a boldly visual joke—a man bestride an enormous dung beetle on a mission to meet god! The spectacle of an actor clinging to the back of some kind of theatrical representation of a beetle mounted on a crane and hoisted above the heads of the audience must have been quite a memorable event.

While Plautus didn't have a large chorus at his disposal, he found other ways to visually advance his stories. It was not uncommon in his plays for characters to adopt disguises, shed them, and then put on new ones.

In *Miles Gloriosus*, one assumes that the larger-than-life braggart soldier has the trappings of the soldier that are either fantastic (visually interesting) or foolish (also visually interesting). Plautus frequently has characters play dress-up, as in *The Persian*, when he has two characters costumed in an exotic fashion to deceive a pimp.

---

7   Aristophanes, *Peace*, ed. Eugene O'Neill Jr. (Perseus Digital Library). www.perseus
.tufts.edu/hopper/text?doc=Perseus:text:1999.01.0038.

Enter SAGARISTIO and the DAUGHTER of SATURIO, from the house, each dressed in Persian costume.

SAGARISTIO

Have I delayed at all?

TOXILUS

Bravo! bravo! dressed out in splendid style. *(to SAGARISTIO)* The tiara does finely set off your dress. Then, too, how beautifully does the slipper become this stranger damsel! But are you thoroughly up in your parts?

SAGARISTIO

Tragedians and Comedians have never been up so well.[8]

Sagaristio concludes this visual display with a sly metatheatrical reference—acknowledging to the audience that they are, in fact, comedians participating in a play.

These visuals employed by our Greek and Roman playwrights are not only meant to entertain or provide the audience with visual stimulation, but are also intended to visually manifest the essential premise of the story. The costuming in *The Wasps* permits the audience to actually experience and understand the litigious nature of Athenian people that Aristophanes critiques in his play. The disguises utilized in *The Persian* offer a commentary on the inability of the pimp, Dordalus, to comprehend—to actually perceive—the true nature of the people he buys and sells in his everyday commerce.

---

8   Plautus, *The Persian*, ed. Henry Thomas Riley (Perseus Digital Library). www.perseus.tufts.edu/hopper/text?doc=Perseus:text:1999.02.0105.

12. THE POETICS OF COMEDY

The plays of ancient Greece and Rome have been translated into many different languages, and as a result are today read and studied around the world, becoming a part of what can only be viewed as a worldwide heritage. Nevertheless, it's inevitable that much of the word craft of the original documents will be lost in translation. This is regrettable because many commentaries inform us just how important the diction of these plays was: the precise selection of words, the rhythms and metres employed in phrasing, the rich use of metaphor, allusions, allegories, and double meanings.

It's important to recall how prized the ancient playwrights were as poets. In *The Frogs* by Aristophanes, when Dionysus must choose between the esteemed playwrights Aeschylus and Euripides, his selection is made to a large degree on the basis of their proficiency in word-crafting. In fact, near the end of the play the character Euripides, for his part, insists that he will "test the plays, word by word"[1] to prove which is the worthier.

One only has to consider the passage below, drawn from Plautus's *Casina*, in its original Latin to sense how rhythm, repetition, and alliteration could be employed to generate something that was a powerful aural experience.

PARADALISCA
Núlla sum, núlla sum, tóta, tota óccidi,
cor metu mortuomst, membra miserae tremunt,
nescio unde auxili, praesidi, perfugi
mi aut opis copiam comparem aut expetam:
tanta factu modo mira miris modis[2]

---

1   Aristophanes, *The Frogs*, ed. Matthew Dillon (Perseus Digital Library). www.perseus.tufts.edu/hopper/text?doc=urn:cts:greekLit:tlg0019.tlg009.perseus-eng1.

2   Plautus, *Casina*, ed. F. Leo (Perseus Digital Library). www.perseus.tufts.edu/hopper/text?doc=Perseus:text:1999.02.0035.

In his commentary on the comic protagonists created by Plautus, William Anderson reflects on the power of the language employed, writing, "These heroes revel in language; they are supremely articulate and love to use words to deceive and to boast of their exploits."[3]

There were many techniques of word craft that the ancient comedians employed, too many to be fully explored in this chapter, but I will attempt to touch on some of the more prominent ones.

I. FIGURES OF SPEECH AND PLAYFUL LANGUAGE

Similes, metaphors, assonances, rhymes, metrical variations, and other literary devices abound in the comic plays of ancient Greece and Rome. Although Aristophanes, Menander, Plautus, and Terence were masterful storytellers in the sense that they intuitively understood matters pertaining to story structure, they were equally proficient wordsmiths, in the sense that they revelled in and applied the distinct and specific richness of the language itself throughout their comedic works. In all of their writings one encounters striking visual constructions. In *The Girl From Samos*, Menander has the Athenian, Demeas, quickly dismiss regions he's visited with a swift visual denunciation, "Pontos! Nothing but fat old men and heaps of fish! And boring business affairs! Byzantium! Just wormwood, everything there bitter!"[4] In *The Eunuch*, Terence has Thais condemn incompetent stewardship with the curt, "You fool! That was trusting the wolf with the lamb!"[5] Plautus visually equates a written contract with a beating written on the body with bruises when in *Pseudolus* he has the clever slave of the same name negotiate with his master, saying, "If we've ever conspired together or embarked on any plot or ever agreed among ourselves about this matter, as when letters are written by pen in a book, then write me black and blue with your elm-wood pen."[6] These vivid

---

3   William Scovil Anderson, *Barbarian Play: Plautus' Roman Comedy* (Toronto: U of Toronto P, 1993), 113.

4   Menander, *The Girl From Samos*, in *The Plays and Fragments*, trans. Maurice Balme (Oxford: Oxford UP, 2001), 49.

5   Terence, *The Eunuch*, trans. ed. Henry Thomas Riley (Perseus Digital Library). http://www.perseus.tufts.edu/hopper/text?doc=Perseus:text:1999.02.0114.

6   Niall W. Slater, *Plautus In Performance* (Princeton: Princeton UP, 1985), 130.

images evoke potent symbols and serve to create a powerful connection between the performance team and the audience.

If the playwrights used words to evoke a striking visual experience, they equally used words to create an auditory experience. Aristophanes was particularly renowned for his creative word construction. Where words didn't exist of sufficient weight or enthusiasm to describe what he imagined, he would simply make them up, as he did in *Lysistrata* when he created the word "*skorodopandokeutriartopolides,*" which translated means roughly "*garlic-primed-inn-keeping-bread-sellers,*" or as he did in *The Knights*, creating the longest word in the Greek language with "*lopadotemachoselachogaleokranioleipsanodrimypotrimmatosilphiopa-ralomelitokatakechymenokicklepikossyphophattoperisteralektryonopten-kephalliokinklopeleiolagoiosiraiobaphetragolopterygon,*" which translated becomes, according to Alan Sommerstein, "*dishy-slicy-sharky-dogfishy-heady-left-oversy-very-strong-saucy-skiphium-bit-salty-honey-poured-overy-thrush-upon-blackbirdy-ringdovey-pigeony-chickeny-roast-cooty-wagtaily-rockdovey-haremeaty-boiled-winy-dippy-diliciousy-wingedy thing.*"[7]

Plautus too was famously fond of fanciful wordplay, and seemed to especially relish the use of alliteration. Duckworth notes a passage in *The Haunted House* that in translation attempts to capture this sensibility, "I've just beheld at the harbor the mightiest mountain of monstrous misery." In *The Two Bacchides*, Plautus plays with sound once again when the clever slave, Chrysalus, concerned that he will be punished with crucifixion by his master says, "I suppose he'll change my name for me the minute he gets back, and transforms me on the spot to Crossalus from Chrysalus."[8]

This granular aspect of writing, the careful attentiveness to the literary skills that render each phrase powerful and maintain a word-by-word connection with the audience, was thoroughly embraced by the comic writers of Greece and Rome.

---

7   James Robson, *Aristophanes: An Introduction* (London: Bloomsbury, 2009), 72.

8   Michael Fontaine, *Funny Words in Plautine Comedy* (Oxford Scholarship Online, 2009). www.oxfordscholarship.com/view/10.1093/acprof:oso/9780195341447.001.0001 /acprof-9780195341447.

II. THE RUNNING GAG

This is a particular tool that is only really effective in longer pieces, as it gathers power with repeated use. One sees it employed in *The Frogs*, as Xanthias complains of his efforts going unacknowledged and unappreciated by Dionysus. So, while Heracles and Dionysus make plans for the journey into Hades, Xanthias interjects bitterly (and repeatedly) that no one spares a thought for him or his pains. Later he is once more overlooked even insofar as getting a seat on Charon's boat to travel into Hades. He complains once more that he has been overlooked as he trudges tiredly to the rendezvous location with their luggage on his shoulders. This repetition and calling attention to his unappreciated status receives payout later when he successfully has his master punished.

Plautus employs running gags in a number of his plays, but in the *The Brothers Menaechmus* he takes this device to another masterful level of proficiency. The continuing joke in this case is one based upon mistaken identity. Two identical twin brothers are separated when they are young when one is abducted. The abducted twin, named Menaechmus, is taken to live in Epidamnus. When the father dies of grief, the grandfather rears the other boy and names him Menaechmus as well, in memory of his kidnapped brother. The two twins, both named Maneachmus, grow up and end up in Epidamnus at the same time. This leads to a series of escalating misunderstandings as they are each, continually, mistaken for the other by their family and servants. This is, at first, understood by the brothers as a mild eccentricity of the citizens of Epidamnus, but gradually, as the play advances, the continued mistakes in identity results in a cumulative payoff, as we see in this latter scene.

THE WIFE OF MENAECHMUS OF EPIDAMNUS
Why, surely, father, I've sent for you not to be my advocate,
but my husband's: on this side you stand, on the other you
plead the cause.

OLD MAN
If he has done wrong in anything, so much the more shall
I censure him than I've censured you. Since he keeps you
provided for and well clothed, and finds you amply in

female servants and provisions, 'tis better, madam, to entertain kindly feelings.

THE WIFE OF MENAECHMUS OF EPIDAMNUS

But he purloins from me gold trinkets and mantles from out of the chests at home; he plunders me, and secretly carries off my ornaments to harlots.

OLD MAN

He does wrong, if he does that; if he does not do it, you do wrong in accusing him when innocent.

THE WIFE OF MENAECHMUS OF EPIDAMNUS

Why at this moment, even, he has got a mantle, father, and a bracelet, which he had carried off to her; now, because I came to know of it, he brings them back.

OLD MAN

I'll know from himself, then, how it happened. I'll go up to this man and accost him. *(goes up to MENAECHMUS)* Tell me this, Menaechmus, what you two are disputing about, that I may know. Why are you pensive? And why does she in anger stand apart from you?

MENAECHMUS SOSICLES

Whoever you are, whatever is your name, old gentleman, I call to witness supreme Jove and the Deities—

OLD MAN

For what reason, or what matter of all matters?

MENAECHMUS SOSICLES

That I have neither done wrong to that woman, who is accusing me of having purloined this *(pointing to the mantle)* away from her at home... and which she solemnly swears that I did take away. If ever I set foot inside of her house where she lives, I wish that I may become the most wretched of all wretched men.

OLD MAN
Are you in your senses to wish this, or to deny that you ever set foot in that house where you live, you downright madman?

MENAECHMUS SOSICLES
Do you say, old gentleman, that I live in this house? *(pointing at the house)*

OLD MAN
Do you deny it?

MENAECHMUS SOSICLES
By my faith, certainly do deny it.

OLD MAN
In your fun you are going too far in denying it; unless you flitted elsewhere this last night. Step this way, please, daughter. *(to the WIFE)* What do you say? Have you removed from this house?

THE WIFE OF MENAECHMUS OF EPIDAMNUS
To what place, or for what reason, prithee?

OLD MAN
I' faith, I don't know.

THE WIFE OF MENAECHMUS OF EPIDAMNUS
He's surely making fun of you.

OLD MAN
Can't you keep yourself quiet? Now, Menaechmus, you really have joked long enough; now do seriously attend to this matter.

MENAECHMUS SOSICLES

Prithee, what have I to do with you? Whence or what person are you? Is your mind right, or hers, in fact, who is an annoyance to me in every way?

THE WIFE OF MENAECHMUS OF EPIDAMNUS

Don't you see how his eyes sparkle? How a green colour is arising on his temples and his forehead; look how his eyes do glisten...

MENAECHMUS SOSICLES

O me! They say I'm mad, whereas they of themselves are mad.

THE WIFE OF MENAECHMUS OF EPIDAMNUS

How he yawns, as he stretches himself. What am I to do now, my father?

OLD MAN

Step this way, my daughter, as far as ever you can from him.

MENAECHMUS SOSICLES

(aside) What is there better for me than, since they say I'm mad, to pretend that I am mad, that I may frighten them away from me? He dances about. Evoë, Bacchus, ho! Bromius, in what forest dost thou invite me to the chase? I hear thee, but I cannot get away from this spot, so much does this raving mad female cur watch me on the left side. And behind there is that other old he-goat, who many a time in his life has proved the destruction of an innocent fellow-citizen by his false testimony.

OLD MAN

(shaking his stick at him) Woe to your head.

MENAECHMUS SOSICLES

Lo! by his oracle, Apollo bids me burn out her eyes with blazing torches. (He points with his fingers at her.)

THE WIFE OF MENAECHMUS OF EPIDAMNUS
I'm undone, my father; he's threatening to burn my
eyes out.

OLD MAN
Hark you, daughter.

THE WIFE OF MENAECHMUS OF EPIDAMNUS
What's the matter? What are we to do?

OLD MAN
What if I call the servants out here? I'll go bring some to
take him away hence, and bind him at home, before he
makes any further disturbance.

MENAECHMUS SOSICLES
(aside) So now; I think now if I don't adopt some plan for
myself, these people will be carrying me off home to their
house. *(aloud)* Dost thou forbid me to spare my fists at all
upon her face, unless she does at once get out of my sight
to utter and extreme perdition? I will do what thou dost
bid me, Apollo. *(runs after her)*

OLD MAN
(to the WIFE) Away with you home as soon as possible,
lest he should knock you down.[9]

What begins as a simple joke—the device of mistaken identity—is applied
and repeated in a series of incrementally more complex and emotion-
ally charged exchanges, until finally at the conclusion of the play the
payout results in the mutual recognition of the long-separated twins, their
reunion, and an ensuing celebration.

9   Plautus, *The Brothers Menaechmus*, ed. Henry Thomas Riley (Perseus Digital
Library). www.perseus.tufts.edu/hopper/text?doc=urn:cts:latinLit:phi0119.phi010
.perseus-eng1.

III. DIRECT ADDRESS AND THE PARABASIS

Direct address, the mechanism by which the convention of the imaginary fourth wall of the theatre is broken and the audience is spoken to directly, is a relatively common device in ancient theatre. The chorus of the Greek theatre regularly warns, advises, admonishes, and shares information with the audience. In many of the ancient works, a prologue establishes the context of the play for the audience, or introduces the theme of the story, and an epilogue or *exode* draws things to a close.

The *parabasis* in particular—that portion of Greek comedy during which the action of the play is set aside and, through the chorus, the playwright is provided the opportunity to share his thoughts with the audience—stands out as a striking example of direct address. These mechanisms allowing actors to step beyond the fourth wall are more formalized and prevalent in the Greek theatre of Old Comedy, but even in the Roman theatre direct address was a frequently used device. "More than one-sixth of Plautus's corpus—and over one-quarter of some plays—is made up of monologues. Though a few monologues include the pretense that characters speak to themselves or think aloud, most must have been addressed explicitly and emphatically to the audience."[10]

Direct address is a fascinating theatrical apparatus. It holds potential to do much more than simply provide information. It can, in a few short lines, provide insights into character, advance a theme, or provide useful information pertaining to plot. It can also offer a kind of metatheatrical ironical commentary or sarcastic observation.

In this opening monologue from *The Brothers Menaechmus*, Peniculus (or Sponge) introduces himself:

PENICULUS
The young men have given me the name of Peniculus, for this reason, because when I eat, I wipe the tables clean... The persons who bind captives with chains, and who put fetters upon runaway slaves, act very foolishly, in my opinion at least. For if bad usage is added to his misfortune

---

10   Timothy J. Moore, *The Theater of Plautus: Playing to the Audience* (Austin: U of Texas P, 1998), 8.

for a wretched man, the greater is his inclination to run away and to do amiss. For by some means or other do they release themselves from the chains; while thus fettered, they either wear away a link with a file, or else with a stone they knock out the nail; 'tis a mere trifle this. He whom you wish to keep securely that he may not run away, with meat and with drink ought he to be chained; do you bind down the mouth of a man to a full table. So long as you give him what to eat and what to drink at his own pleasure in abundance every day, i' faith he'll never run away, even if he has committed an offence that's capital; easily will you secure him so long as you shall bind him with such chains. So very supple are these chains of food, the more you stretch them so much the more tightly do they bind. But now I'm going directly to Menaechmus; whither for this long time I have been sentenced, thither of my own accord I am going, that he may enchain me. For, by my troth, this man does not nourish persons, but he quite rears and reinvigorates them; no one administers medicine more agreeably. Such is this young man; himself with a very well-stocked larder, he gives dinners fit for Ceres; so does he heap the tables up, and piles so vast of dishes does he arrange, you must stand on your couch if you wish for anything at the top. But I have now had an interval these many days, while I've been lording it at home all along together with my dear ones;—for nothing do I eat or purchase but what it is most dear. But inasmuch as dear ones, when they are provided, are in the habit of forsaking us, I am now paying him a visit. But his door is opening; and see, I perceive Menaechmus himself; he is coming out of doors.[11]

In this selection, Plautus creates a prologue that simultaneously serves many functions. He entertains by employing delightfully visual literary

---

11   Plautus, *The Brothers Menaechmus*, ed. Henry Thomas Riley (Perseus Digital Library). www.perseus.tufts.edu/hopper/text?doc=urn:cts:latinLit:phi0119.phi010 .perseus-eng1.

exaggeration: "So very supple are these chains of food" and "so does he heap the tables up, and piles so vast of dishes does he arrange, you must stand on your couch if you wish for anything at the top." In a few deft, broad strokes, Plautus establishes the rough parameters of the character. By having him directly address the audience, he permits Peniculus to draw the audience into his confidence, and by doing so makes them his accomplices.

If the *parabasis* of Old Comedy is a device no longer commonly employed by writers, it is at the same time a very clear and direct precursor to the monologist and stand-up comic who are very familiar with audiences today. Like the stand-up comic, the *parabasis* adopts an attitude and addresses problems of society or political peculiarities in a comic vein.

The *parabasis* of *Peace* by Aristophanes presents precisely this kind of commentary.

> Undoubtedly the comic poet who mounted the stage to praise himself in the parabasis would deserve to be handed over to the sticks or the beadles. Nevertheless, oh Muse, if it be right to esteem the most honest and illustrious of our comic writers at his proper value, permit our poet to say that he thinks he has deserved a glorious renown. First of all, he is the one who has compelled his rivals no longer to scoff at rags or to war with lice; and as for those Heracleses, always chewing and ever hungry, he was the first to cover them with ridicule and to chase them from the stage; he has also dismissed that slave, whom one never failed to set weeping before you, so that his comrade might have the chance of jeering at his stripes and might ask, "Wretch, what has happened to your hide? Has the lash rained an army of its thongs on you and laid your back waste?" After having delivered us from all these wearisome ineptitudes and these low buffooneries, he has built up for us a great art, like a palace with high towers, constructed of fine phrases, great thoughts and of jokes not common on the streets. Moreover it's not obscure private persons or women that he stages in his comedies; but, bold as Heracles, it's the very greatest whom he attacks, undeterred by the fetid stink of leather or the threats of hearts of mud. He has the right to say, "I am the first ever dared to go straight

for that beast with the sharp teeth and the terrible eyes that
flashed lambent fire like those of Cynna, surrounded by a
hundred lewd flatterers, who spittle-licked him to his heart's
content; it had a voice like a roaring torrent, the stench of a
seal, the unwashed balls of a Lamia and the arse of a camel.
I did not recoil in horror at the sight of such a monster, but
fought him relentlessly to win your deliverance and that of
the islanders." Such are the services which should be graven
in your recollection and entitle me to your thanks. Yet I have
not been seen frequenting the wrestling school intoxicated
with success and trying to seduce young boys; but I took all
my theatrical gear and returned straight home. I pained folk
but little and caused them much amusement; my conscience
rebuked me for nothing.[12]

The employment of exaggeration, the sarcastic observations upon life
and character, the bravado, and the casual sprinkling of vulgarity are
all elements one can observe in the comic routines at nightclubs or on
television today.

In its sharing of indelicate observations it eschews the politenesses
and formality associated with exchanges between strangers and instead
demands a kind of familiarity. The *parabasis* of Aristophanes goes a step
further, portraying those outside the speaker's "inner circle" as unintel-
ligent, vulgar, and base, and invites the audience to symbolically join the
speaker as part of a select group who are informed, clever, and sophis-
ticated. The informality of the approach declares each individual in the
audience a confederate and friend, and invites them to come to the same
conclusions that the playwright does.

The prologues and asides use many of the same strategies that contemporary comedians employ—satire, exaggeration, and imitation. And in
many ways they both achieve the same end, permitting the audience to
understand the world—and the speaker—in a new way.

12   Aristophanes, *Peace*, ed. Daniel Stevenson (Project Gutenberg, 2008).
www.gutenberg.org/files/2571/2571-h/2571-h.htm.

IV. MULTIPLE PLOTS

In her chapter on *The Brothers Menaechmus*, Professor Elaine Fantham opines that it "is perhaps the most satisfying among all the plays of Plautus in the balance and symmetry of its structure. There is not only the symmetry of alternation between the resident, Epidamnian Menaechmus, and his brother, the Stranger from Syracuse—that is, a balanced grouping of scenes for each hero in turn."[13] In this play, and in others arising out of the New Comedy, we begin to see the potential that emerges out of developing two related stories simultaneously. This process embraces the potential for comparing and contrasting character, and by so doing arriving at a better and richer understanding of both characters. There is also the potential for adding further complication to the essential plot of the play, and consequently developing a more sustained, emotional build and a subsequently more powerful climax and payoff. There is nothing like this narrative architecture that exists in Old Comedy—at least as far as we know—but in New Comedy this construction seems very welcome, and was thoroughly embraced by the Roman comics.

Terence is particularly well known for developing multiple plots simultaneously. As Peter Brown notes in his collection of Terence's works, "He has become famous for his 'double plots,' since all his plays except *The Mother-in-Law* display the varied fortunes of two young men in love, and many other contrasting pairs of characters are also to be found."[14] This excerpt from *The Brothers* offers a clear view of the structure of this kind of paralleling development.

    DEMEA
    What has he done! a wretch whom neither fear,
    Nor modesty, nor any law can bind!
    For not to speak of all his former pranks,
    What has he been about but even now!

---

13   Elaine Fantham, *Roman Readings: Roman Response to Greek Literature from Plautus to Statius and Quintilian* (Berlin: Walter de Gruyter, 2011), 3.

14   Peter Brown, *Terence: The Comedies* (New York: Oxford UP, 2006), vii.

MICIO
What has he done?

DEMEA
Burst open doors, and made
His way by force into another's house;
Half-kill'd the master and his family,
And carried off a wench whom he was fond of.
All Athens cries out shame upon him for it.
I have been told of it a hundred times
Since my arrival. 'Tis the town-talk, Micio.
And if we needs must draw comparisons,
Does not he see his brother thrifty, sober,
Attentive to his business in the country?
Not given to these practices; and when
I say all this to him, to you I say it.
You are his ruin, Micio.

MICIO
How unjust
Is he who wants experience! who believes
Nothing is right but what he does himself!

DEMEA
Why d'ye say that?

MICIO
Because you, Demea,
Misjudge these matters. 'Tis no heinous crime
For a young man to wench or drink—'tis not,
Believe me!—nor to force doors open—this,
If neither you nor I have done, it was
That poverty allow'd us not. And now
You claim a merit to yourself, from that
Which want constrain'd you to. It is not fair.
For had there been but wherewithal to do't,
We likewise should have done thus. Wherefore you,

Were you a man, would let your younger son,
Now, while it suits his age, pursue his pleasures;
Rather than, when it less becomes his years,
When, after wishing long, he shall at last
Be rid of you, he should run riot then.

DEMEA

Oh Jupiter! the man will drive me mad.
Is it no crime, d'ye say, for a young man
To take these courses?

MICIO

Nay, nay; do but hear me,
Nor stun me with the self-same thing forever!
Your elder son you gave me for adoption:
He's mine, then, Demea; and if he offends,
'Tis an offense to me, and I must bear
The burden. Does he treat? or drink? or dress?
'Tis at my cost. —Or wench? I will supply him,
While 'tis convenient to me; when 'tis not,
His mistresses perhaps will shut him out.
—Has he broke open doors? we'll make them good.
Or torn a coat? it shall be mended. I,
Thank Heaven, have enough to do all this,
And 'tis as yet not irksome. —In a word,
Have done, or chuse some arbiter between us:
I'll prove that you are more in fault than I.

DEMEA

Ah, learn to be a father; learn from those
Who know what 'tis to be indeed a parent!

MICIO

By nature you're his father, I by counsel.

DEMEA

You! do you counsel any thing?

MICIO
Nay, nay;
If you persist, I'm gone.

DEMEA
Is't thus you treat me?

MICIO
Must I be plagued with the same thing so often?

DEMEA
It touches me.

MICIO
And me it touches too.
But, Demea, let us each look to our own;
Let me take care of one, and mind you t'other.
For to concern yourself with both, appears
As if you'd redemand the boy you gave.

DEMEA
Ah, Micio!

MICIO
So it seems to me.

DEMEA
Well, well;
Let him, if 'tis your pleasure, waste, destroy.
And squander; it is no concern of mine.
If henceforth I e'er say one word—[15]

In this passage, it is possible to detect the careful, deliberate construction of the double plot. Not only are two very different brothers introduced,

---

15   Terence, *The Brothers*, trans. George Colman (U of Adelaide). https://ebooks
.adelaide.edu.au/t/terence/adelphoe/complete.html.

but the essential differences between them are established, as well as the root cause for their conflict. Simultaneous to this is developed the faint image of the two different brothers—the sons, not seen, but only mentioned—and the audience understands that their activities and characters will be observed and judged as well. The intricate twining of these two stories permits an enormous amount of information to be shared swiftly.

The essential strength of the double plot is the ability to advance a related theme in different directions and at the same time sustain dramatic tension. From these beginnings on the Greek and Roman stages emerged the jump cut device so popular today in television and film, where the narrative leaps from one story to another, holding the one narrative thread taut while continuing to weave other narrative threads in and out. The attention of the audience is held in suspense as the focus leaps from one story to the next.

V. MUSICALITY

An aspect that is almost entirely lost to contemporary readers is the musicality of the text of the ancient comedies. We know that a great deal of what was presented by the Greek and Roman comedians was sung, but do not know, nor perhaps ever will know, how the plays sounded. That may be lost to us forever.

The instruments that most commonly accompanied the actors were the tibia or aulos (a wind instrument), the kithara (a kind of lyre), and timpani (a kind of drum), as well as various other percussive instruments including cymbals. We have a sense, knowing that the metre of the text changed according to the emotional tenor of the piece, that the music was truly composed to complement and drive the narrative content. How the music was integrated into the telling of the story is a question that has vexed subsequent writers. Consider just reading the libretto of an opera today, or reading only the book of a contemporary musical and think about what an incomplete experience that would be.

The long choral speeches so prevalent in Greek theatre, and the longer monologues that occur in both Greek and Roman theatre often seem curiously static to the modern reader, but if we imagine them sung it's possible to view them completely differently. It was in attempting to respond to these challenges that the form of opera emerged many, many years later, and from opera, the genre of musical theatre.

CONCLUSION

Reading the plays of Aristophanes, Menander, Plautus, and Terence is like viewing a film through an ancient projector that only partially works. Images are one moment clear and crisp, the next vague and barely recognizable. The humour of some portions is so instantly apparent and immediate, so *funny*, that the texts feel curiously modern. Other portions remain ambiguous, inexplicable, or only partially realized. Both the clear and the unclear offer opportunities to the modern writer.

The immediately approachable components of these past works remind those of us writing today that certain comedic elements hold universality. When we laugh at the cleverness of a servant outwitting his master,

The Theatre of Epidaurus offers a vision of classic Greek theatre design.

we are reminded that every culture possesses its own pecking order, and we detect an echo of our own social disparities and inequalities in these representations from the past. The mad, obsessive desires and passions that drive comic characters in the Greek and Roman theatre equally fuel the decisions and actions of individuals walking among us today. We are reminded that the braggarts, blowhards, misers, and lotharios of our world are ripe for lampooning.

Those portions of the comic works that feel ambiguous or unclear present contemporary writers with a different kind of challenge. The task becomes to investigate and determine how the obscure passages of past productions amused and entertained their audiences. The texts alone may not offer solutions. In the same way that contemporary opera emerged as an active attempt to understand the challenges of ancient written works, so may other solutions emerge to clarify passages that presently appear impenetrable. In recent years there has been interesting work done with choruses as modern directors struggled to make sense of those long, unwieldy, seemingly static passages of text. New ways of performing the chorus have been explored, and those dramatic units that once seemed so resolutely inert are now regarded as more flexible and dynamic. What other theatrical solutions may emerge as additional study is devoted to these historical documents? What other portions will suddenly pop into focus?

One thing quickly becomes apparent when you read the works of the ancient comedians—throughout history comic writers have struggled with the same challenges that writers have always struggled with. How does one capture a story in a way that seems fresh? How can one create characters that compel? What will make a restive audience remain attentive, and what will make them *laugh*? The Greek and Roman comedians accomplished all these things in spades, and in so doing developed a vocabulary that the comic theatre has employed ever since. Stock characters, physical comedy, comic asides, romantic comedy, parallel plots—these concepts emerged as the Greeks and Romans rehearsed, sang, and danced at the great theatre festivals of their times.

The stories the Greek and Roman playwrights wrote reflected their willingness to embrace everything human on a large scale—large characters, extreme passions, sexuality, greed, pride, cowardice. At the same time, these seemingly lighthearted plays made room to accommodate moments of genuine tenderness, intimacy, and darkness as well. The ancient comedy was, in short, a form full of contradictions and paradoxes and, ultimately, it leaves us in the present with our own paradox. Before we can truly move forward, perhaps we must first take a long look back.

THE END

APPENDIX A
TIMELINE OF THE DEVELOPMENT
OF COMEDIC THEATRE

c. 546–527 BCE   The tyrant of Athens, Pisistratus, founds the annual Festival of the Greater Dionysia.

c. 540 BCE   Comic playwright Epicharmus of Kos is born. Although no examples of his work exist today, his are believed to be among the earliest comic plays to have been based upon a plot.

c. 536–533 BCE   Actor/producer Thespis performs tragedy at the Festival of the Greater Dionysia in Athens. He is reputed to be the first to introduce an actor separate from the chorus in his work.

c. 500 BCE   Greek playwright Pratinus of Phlius initiates the Satyr play in Athens.

498 BCE   The initial construction of the Theatre of Dionysus in Athens is completed.

c. 486–460 BCE   The first comic plays are introduced to the Greater Dionysia festival.

c. 446 BCE   Birth of the Greek comic playwright Aristophanes. His plays represent the only surviving example of Greek Old Comedy.

c. 450 BCE	Death of Epicharmus.
425 BCE	*The Acharnians* by Aristophanes, the earliest comic play in existence today, is first performed.
388 BCE	*Plutus*, the latest play written by Aristophanes in existence today, is first performed.
c. 380 BCE	Death of Aristophanes.
c. 342 BCE	Birth of Greek comic poet Menander. His work represents the only surviving example of Greek New Comedy.
335 BCE	Aristotle's *Poetics* is written, a document that examines, among other things, what theatre is. This document will have far-reaching influence on Western theatre. Comic theatre is mentioned, albeit only briefly.
325–146 BCE	The Hellenistic Period. A time of significant Greek influence in Europe, Africa, and Asia following the conquests of Alexander the Great and his subsequent death. During this time, Greek theatre is widely disseminated. Many Greek-style theatres are built in those areas that have been conquered and colonized. Guilds of performers tour this area, presenting plays and presiding over rituals associated with the theatre.
316 BCE	*Dyskolos* (*The Grouch*) by Menander, the sole intact example of Greek New Comedy, is first performed.
c. 291 BCE	Death of Menander.
c. 254 BCE	Birth of comic playwright Titus Maccius Plautus. His works are the earliest example existing today of Roman comic theatre.

200 BCE	*Stichus*, written by Plautus, is performed. It's not possible to firmly date the performance of all of the plays by Plautus, but of the plays existing today, this is the earliest that can be conclusively dated.
c. 195 BCE	Birth of comic playwright Publius Terentius Afer (Terence).
191 BCE	*Pseudolus* by Plautus is performed. The latest of his plays, as far as can be determined.
c. 184 BCE	Death of Plautus.
166 BCE	*Andria* by Terence is performed, the first of his plays.
163 BCE	*Heauton Timorumenos* by Terence is performed, the last of his plays.
c. 159 BCE	Death of Terence.
55 BCE	The first permanent Roman theatre built of stone is dedicated—the Theatre of Pompey.
30 BCE–476 CE	The era of the Roman Empire. As countries are conquered and settled by the Romans, Roman-style theatres are built, plays are widely performed, and the comic form takes root throughout the empire.

APPENDIX B
SYNOPSES

THE WORKS OF ARISTOPHANES

1. Akharneis (*The Acharnians*) An Athenian citizen named Dikaeopolis is enormously frustrated with the difficulties that arise from the continuing war between Athens and Sparta. He arrives at the Pnyx, where, when the Assembly meets, he hopes to convince Athenian politicians to see reason and arrange a cessation of conflict. They refuse to listen to him, however, so Dikaeopolis decides to take an unconventional approach and strike his own separate truce. Soon, others are looking on enviously as he enjoys the fruits of his own independent peace treaty.

2. Hippeis (*The Knights*) In this allegorical play, Aristophanes pokes fun at his contemporary Cleon, a local politician whom he accuses of warmongering and corruption. At the very outset of the play, two servants of Demos (the People) complain of a high-ranking servant, the Paphlagonian (Cleon's literary parallel), whom they allege is a tyrant. They consult an oracle and learn that a sausage seller will defeat him. Moments later, a sausage seller, Agoracritus, appears. They convince him to contest the Paphlagonian and the two debate and shout in an outrageous fashion, eventually petitioning their differences before Demos. Ultimately Agoracritus proves successful and the Paphlagonian is deposed.

3. Nephelai (*The Clouds*) Strepsiades, an Athenian citizen, is troubled and unable to sleep because of the debts incurred by his free-spending wife and son. He attempts to convince his son to enrol in a philosophy school so that the son, Pheidippides, will learn how to make compelling arguments, becoming able to defeat those who hold their debts in court. Pheidippides rejects this plan, so Strepsiades decides to enrol instead. He goes to the school and meets a student who demonstrates some of the important research that the master of the school—Socrates—has been involved in. Strepsiades asks to meet Socrates, and within moments encounters the great man. Socrates arrives, suspended in a basket so that he can view the sky and all the phenomena of the sky—including the clouds of the title. The Clouds (the chorus) sing to Strepsiades and indicate that he will do well at the school, but ultimately he proves to be a very poor student. Strepsiades returns to his son and again insists that he enrol. Grudgingly, Pheidippides goes to the school and emerges from it with the necessary training. This proves a double-edged sword. He easily dismisses the debtors that have plagued his father, but he also beats his father and argues that this is completely justified. Disillusioned with the school, Strepsiades attacks it and sets it aflame.

4. Sphekes (*The Wasps*) Philocleon is a man obsessed with attending the courts and viewing legal proceedings. So overwhelming is this obsession that the rest of his life—his hygiene and health—have fallen by the wayside. His son, Bdelycleon, attempts to prevent him from leaving his house, but some of Philocleon's colleagues (the wasps of the play) from the courthouse arrive and try to free him. Bdelycleon manages to keep his father home, and as an inducement permits Philocleon to offer mock court-room sessions in the house. When Bdelycleon brings his father to a party afterwards, his father embarrasses him by drinking too much and insulting the guests. The chorus commiserates with Bdelycleon, observing that it is difficult for the old to change their ways.

5. Eirene (*Peace*) Trygaeus, a native of Athens, frustrated at the continuing war between Athens and Sparta, decides to mount an enormous dung beetle and fly it into the heavens to confront Zeus and plead for peace. He discovers that the gods have abandoned heaven, and a giant named War has imprisoned Peace, Harvest, and Festival. Trygaeus overhears War say that he intends to destroy the Greeks utterly. When War exits, Trygaeus gathers some help and frees Peace and her colleagues. He then marries Harvest and brings about a cessation of conflicts. Celebrations ensue.

6. Ornithes (*The Birds*) Two citizens of Athens, Pisthetaerus and Euelpides, disillusioned with the litigious nature of Athenian society and seeking a place of refuge where they can escape some bad debts they've incurred, attempt to find and take council from Tereus, a man who has been transformed into a bird. They find him and as they discuss what they might do or where they might go, Pisthetaerus conceives of a plan through which the birds might place an embargo on the sacrifices that are sent through burnt offerings to the gods, and by doing this achieve a position of power and privilege. Tereus convenes a council of the birds, who at first are alarmed at seeing men in their midst. They attack Pisthetaerus and Euelpides, but once Tereus convinces them to listen to the men the birds are persuaded that the plan is a good one. The birds then prevent sacrifices from rising to the gods, and by the conclusion of the play a new order of bird supremacy has been established. Pisthetaerus and Euelpides are lauded and celebrations are held.

7. Lysistrate (*Lysistrata*) Lysistrata convenes women representatives of Sparta and Boeotia and convinces them that the only way the war between Athens and Sparta can be brought to an end is if women compel men to make peace. Lysistrata outlines a novel strategy to force men to agree to their demands—a sex strike. The women agree that they will refrain from sexual relations with any man until a peace treaty is concluded, and at the same time they will occupy the Acropolis to demonstrate their serious intentions. The men, surprised and angered by these actions, try to retake the Acropolis but fail, and at the same time they grow increasingly sexually frustrated. At last the men send a delegation to speak with Lysistrata who argues persuasively on behalf of peace. A peace treaty is struck and celebrations ensue.

8. Thesmophoriazusae (*The Women Celebrating the Thesmophoria*) Euripides, the celebrated Greek playwright, expresses concern that women, angered at him because of his unflattering portrayals of the opposite sex in his plays, will meet at the Festival of Thesmophoria and devise a plan to kill him. He arranges to have a relative, Mnesilochus, disguise himself as a woman, sneak into the gathering, and covertly observe the proceedings. Unfortunately, Mnesilochus's cover is blown and he is seized and arrested. Euripides arrives just in time, informs the Assembly that he will modify his portrayals of women, and frees Mnesilochus.

9. **Batrakhoi** (*The Frogs*) Dionysus and his servant descend into Hades to fetch back a poet who will restore Athens to its previous glory. Dionysus intends to bring back Euripides, but once there he discovers Aeschylus and Euripides in a contest. He presides over the competition and ends up bringing Aeschylus back.

10. **Ecclesiazousae** (*The Assemblywomen*) A group of Athenian women, led by Praxagora, decide that they could rule Athens better than the men. They disguise themselves as men, attend the Assembly, and promote and vote for a measure that will give women power. Once this measure is passed, the women institute a program of strict equality. Athenian's physical needs are taken care of completely—everyone receives adequate food and housing. Other more radical measures accompany these, however. All property is centralized, and every man, before he may enjoy sexual relations with a younger, more attractive woman, must first have sexual relations with an older, less attractive woman.

11. **Plutus** (*Wealth*) Chremylos, an elderly Athenian citizen, travels to Delphi to solicit advice from the divine oracle. The oracle instructs him to follow the first man he meets upon his return to Athens and invite him home. Although this individual seems to be a blind beggar, he in fact turns out to be the god of wealth. Chremylos has the god's vision restored to him, causing enormous unintended consequences. Suddenly the god bestows his blessing on the deserving, rather than randomly upon the deserving and undeserving alike. The goddess of poverty appears and rebukes Chremylos, pointing out that now workers will not work, because they will no longer feel the necessity. Hermes then arrives and informs Chremylos that the gods are unhappy as well, since mortals now sacrifice only to Wealth and not the other gods. Worried about his condition in the new heavens, Hermes offers to serve Chremylos. Chremylos suggests that Wealth should be installed in a place of prominence in the temples, and they march off to do so.

THE WORKS OF MENANDER

12. Dyskolos (*The Grouch*) Pan appears and tells the audience that he intends to reward Knemon's daughter for her devotion to him. He plans to have a wealthy young man, Sostratos, fall in love with her. Sostratos appears in short order—smitten by Knemon's daughter—and attempts to arrange a marriage. Knemon, the father and the grouch of this play, only wishes to be left alone. He deters, runs off, and beats any strangers who approach his door and he completely rebuffs all solicitations on behalf of Sostratos. When Knemon accidentally falls into a well, however, and is rescued by Sostratos, the old man realizes the error of his ways and agrees to permit the marriage to proceed. He is taught a rough lesson in proper social behaviour and is compelled to attend the wedding festivities.

THE PLAYS OF PLAUTUS

13. Amphitruo (*Amphitryon*) An unusual play for Plautus, *Amphitryon* develops a mythical storyline. The great god Jupiter wishes to have sex with Alcmena, who is both a beautiful mortal and married. To achieve his goal, Jupiter changes his appearance so that he resembles Alcmena's husband, Amphitryon. The real Amphitryon is returning from a war and sends his slave, Sosia, ahead to prepare his household. Mercury, acting on behalf of Jupiter, changes his shape so that he resembles Sosia. When the real Sosia arrives, he meets the faux Sosia, batters him, and sends him away. The real Amphitryon arrives the next day, confused by the story his slave has told him. He meets with his wife, who is also confused because, as far as she knows, she and her husband made love only a short time ago. Amphitryon becomes angry when his wife tells him this and begins to suspect her of adultery. Alcmena, upset at these accusations, prepares to leave. Jupiter returns, reveals what occurred, and informs Amphitryon that his wife will give birth to twins—one Amphitryon's and one Jupiter's (who will grow up to become the hero Hercules). Amphitryon and Alcmena express their gratitude for being so honoured by a god.

14. Asinaria (*The Asses*) Argyrippus is a young Athenian in love with a courtesan named Philaenium. Her mother/procuress, Cleareta, has made it plain that Argyrippus will not receive access to Philaenium unless he provides twenty minæ, which Argyrippus doesn't have. Demaenetus, his aged father, wants to help his son out, but his wife, Artemona, controls the finances in the family. Demaenetus has two slaves, Libanus and Leonida, develop a plan to cheat his wife of the payment she's to receive for the sale of several asses. They execute the plan and attain the necessary funds to purchase Philaenium, but Demaenetus places an addendum on the agreement. He informs his son that he wishes to enjoy the favours of Philaenium prior to his son. Argyrippus regretfully agrees. Artemona is informed of these goings-on, and as Argyrippus, Philaenium, and Demaenetus enjoy a meal together, she arrives in a state of fury. She berates Demaenetus in the most scathing terms and sends him home, leaving Philaenium alone with Argyrippus.

15. Aulularia (*The Pot of Gold*) A miserly old man, Euclio, has discovered a pot of gold. He keeps it hidden, never uses a coin of it, and frets every day that someone will steal it, changing its hiding place frequently. His wealthy neighbour approaches him and asks if he might marry his daughter. This alliance strikes Euclio as risky, because it will bring others into his life who might rob him of his gold. He hides and rehides his gold, but ultimately a slave spies Euclio as he moves the gold and steals it. Euclio becomes frantic to recover it. Lyconides, master of the slave who stole the gold, confesses to having made Euclio's daughter pregnant. He compels his slave to return the gold, and he in turn is permitted to marry Euclio's daughter.

16. Bacchides (*The Two Bacchides*) Two prostitutes, both named Bacchis, draw the ardent attention of two friends, Mnesilochus and Pistoclerus. Mnesilochus asks Chrysalus, his father's slave, to help him raise the funds necessary to purchase the freedom of his Bacchis. Chrysalus tricks Mnesilochus's father, Nicobulus, into providing these funds. Mnesilochus learns of Pistoclerus's love for a Bacchis, and thinking that it is the girl he is in love with, becomes angry and hurt. Mnesilochus confesses to his father that he was tricked and returns the funds. Then, Mnesilochus discovers that there are, in fact, *two* sisters named Bacchis and that Pistoclerus is interested in the *other* Bacchis. Mnesilochus returns to Chrysalus and once again asks for his help. Chrysalus once more connives to get the money from Nicobulus. Nicobulus learns that he has been deceived, and, angered, goes with Pistoclerus's father to the brothel where Bacchis and Bacchis work. The girls exert their charms and the old men are not only mollified, but convinced to enter the brothel.

17. Captivi (*The Captives*) Hegio, a wealthy citizen of Aetolia, has purchased several prisoners of a war with Ellis. Of these prisoners, two receive special attention in the play: a high-ranking individual named Philocrates and his servant Tyndarus. Hegio plans to send Tyndarus back to Ellis, where he will arrange an exchange of Philocrates for Hegio's son, Philipolemus. But Philocrates and Tyndarus exchange identities, and Hegio ends up sending Philocrates instead. Tyndarus, in the meantime, remains behind and maintains the illusion that he is a high-ranking citizen of Ellis. His true identity is accidentally revealed, however, by another prisoner of Ellis. Infuriated by what he perceives as treachery, Hegio places heavy chains on Tyndarus and sends him to the quarries. Ultimately Philocrates returns with Philipolemus, to free Tyndarus in exchange, and it is then revealed through a surprising twist of events that Tyndarus is in fact Hegio's long-lost other son, who was kidnapped many years back.

18. Casina (*Casina*) Lysidamus and his wife have a servant in their employ named Casina. This girl, abandoned at their door as a baby and raised in their household, has since grown up to be quite a beauty. Now, Lysidamus's son Euthynicus wants to marry her. Lysidamus has other, more venal plans in mind, however. He intends for Casina to marry Olympio, his servant, so that Lysidamus will, through Olympio, be permitted sexual relations with her without his wife knowing. Cleostrata uncovers these plans and sets up an elaborate counter-plan to defeat—and humiliate—her husband.

19. Cistellaria (*The Casket*) Phanostrata bears the child of an illicit union then gives it to her servant, Lampadiscus, to abandon. The child is rescued and taken in by Melaenis, who names the infant Silenium, and raises her. Melaenis retains a casket within which are contained items that Silenium wore when she was first abandoned. Demipho, the father of Silenium, eventually marries Phanostrata, and together they try to find their daughter. Ultimately, the casket is dropped to the ground and the interior materials exposed, providing the evidence that Silenium is the long-lost daughter, and the family is at last reunited.

20. **Curculio** (*Curculio*) In this, Plautus's shortest existing play, Phaedromus yearns for Planesium, who is owned by the procurer Cappadox. Phaedromus doesn't have the money necessary to purchase her, so he sends Curculio to borrow the funds. Curculio is unsuccessful in this regard, but he encounters a soldier named Therapontigonus who also expresses a desire to purchase Planesium. Curculio, thinking on his feet, steals Therapontigonus's ring. He then forges a letter requesting money from a banker, using the seal from the ring to confirm the identity. Following this, he purchases Planesium and brings her to Phaedromus. Therapontigonus arrives in a foul mood, but the ring has also revealed Planesium is actually freeborn and his sister. Consequently, the funds are returned to Therapontigonus, and Planesium and Phaedromus marry.

21. **Epidicus** (*Epidicus*) Epidicus, the slave after whom the play is named, attempts to help his master's son, Stratippocles, attain the object of his affection, a female slave named Acropolistis. To do this he must first trick his master, Periphanes, into providing him with the necessary funds. Epidicus convinces Periphanes that the money is required to free his long-lost daughter, who has been captured and carried to Athens and Periphanes gives Epidicus the required funding. Stratippocles, however, while off on a campaign, falls for a new and different woman. He borrows money to purchase her. When he returns he directs Epidicus to get more money so that he may pay off this debt. Epidicus turns to Periphanes once more. He convinces Periphanes that his son has become infatuated with a singing girl. Epidicus argues that the only way to keep Stratippocles from marrying her is by purchasing her. Again, Periphanes is relieved of his money. Epidicus pays off the outstanding loan that Stratippocles had incurred and then purchases a faux singing girl. As might be expected, considerable confusion results, and at one point it looks like Epidicus will be punished for his double-dealing. Eventually, the real long-lost daughter is reunited with her father, Stratippocles and Acropolistis get together, and, as a reward for his efforts, which are considerable, Epidicus is freed.

22. Menaechmi (*The Brothers Menaechmus*) Two twin boys, Menaechmus and Sosicles, are separated when their father elects to take only one, Sosicles, with him on a distant business venture. While they are away from their native city of Syracuse, the other twin is seized by a businessman, taken away, and raised in Epidamnus. Their natural father perishes, leaving their grandfather to raise Sosicles, but elects to rename him Menaechmus in memory of the lost brother. As the Syracusan Menaechmus matures he elects to search for his lost brother. He stops over in Epidamnus, and before long there are a series of mistaken identities as various members of the Epidamnus Menaechmus inner circle begin to apprehend the Syracusan Menaechmus for their own. These mistakes multiply and grow increasingly complex, until finally the two brothers actually meet, recognize one another, and are reunited.

23. Mercator (*The Merchant*) A young Athenian, Charinus, during his travels abroad on business, falls in love with Pasicompsa. He brings her home as his mistress, but doesn't wish to let his father, Demipho, know. When the boat docks, Demipho arrives, sees Pasicompsa, and develops a romantic interest in her as well. Charinus's slave, Acanthio, aware that Charinus doesn't want his father to know the truth, tells Demipho that Pasicompsa has been purchased to serve as a slave for Charinus's mother. At this point Demipho, desiring Pasicompsa but not wanting his wife to know, says he is going to sell the girl. Both Charinus and Demipho have proxies prepared to purchase Pasicompsa, but Demipho is successful. His proxy, Lysimachus, takes Pasicompsa home on behalf of Demipho, where Lysimachus's wife discovers her and thinks he is having an affair. Ultimately, Charinus learns where Pasicompsa is, Demipho learns that Charinus really is in love with Pasicompsa, and Demipho abandons his plans to own the girl himself.

24. Miles Gloriosus (*The Braggart Soldier*) A young Athenian named Pleusicles loves a courtesan named Philocomasium, but a boastful captain by the name of Pyrgopolinices carries Philocomasium to Ephesus. By chance, Pleusicles's servant, Palaestrio, is captured by pirates and sold to the same Pyrgopolinices. The wily Palaestrio contacts Pleusicles and tells him to come to Ephesus. Once he is there, Palaestrio contacts and hires two courtesans to act out a play within a play in which Acroteleutium pretends to be a rich wife who is infatuated with Pyrgopolinices, and her servant negotiates an affair. Pyrgopolinices releases Philocomasium so that he will be able to devote himself to Acroteleutium. He gives Palaestrio to Philocomasium as a gift to keep her happy and Palaestrio, Philocomasium, and Pleusicles swiftly depart together on a ship. Pyrgopolinices is assailed by the neighbour pretending to be the offended husband of Acroteleutium and the braggart is then beaten, humbled, and corrected.

25. Mostellaria (*The Haunted House*) Philolaches, a young Athenian, leads a dissolute life while his father is out of town. He has borrowed a considerable amount of money to finance his partying and to purchase the freedom of his mistress, Philematium. He and his friends are in the midst of carousing when Philolaches's slave Tranio runs on, announcing that Philolache's father has returned from his business trip and will arrive shortly. The group is too inebriated to formulate a clear plan, so Tranio instructs Philolaches to go into the house, lock the door, and remain quiet. When Theuropides arrives, Tranio convinces him that his house has become haunted, and consequently has been abandoned. He urges the old man to flee before a spectral curse falls upon him. Theuropides exits, but returns shortly after consulting with the individual who sold him the house. This person knows nothing about any haunting. At the same time Theuropides returns, the banker who loaned Philolaches his money arrives, looking to receive repayment. Tranio invents yet another story, telling Theuropides that his son borrowed the money to purchase another home—the one next door. Theuropides is satisfied that this is a good investment, but wants to inspect the house. Tranio arranges for an inspection, but ultimately he is unable to sustain the fabrication and the truth emerges. Theuropides, angered at being deceived, seeks to punish Tranio, and Tranio is compelled to seek refuge at a holy altar. Tranio is saved when a friend of Philolaches provides funds to repay the debts, and everyone is forgiven their transgressions.

26. Persa (*The Persian*) Toxilus, a servant whose master is presently absent, elects to free the object of his desire, Lemniselene, from the procurer, Dordalus. He tries to borrow money for this purpose, but none of his friends have sufficient funds. However, Toxilus devises a plan. He convinces an acquaintance, Saturio, to have his daughter disguise herself as a

Persian slave. He then sells her to Dordalus, and with the fee he acquires from this transaction, he purchases Lemniselene's freedom. Once he has secured Lemniselene's liberty, he has Saturio make an appearance as a grieved father claiming that his daughter is freeborn and unavailable for sale. He has the money that was paid for Lemniselene returned and celebrations follow.

27. Poenulus (*The Carthaginian*) Agorastocles was originally from Carthage, but was purchased, adopted, and now lives in Calydon. He has fallen in love with a slave, also a former Carthaginian, named Adelphasium. She and her sister, Anterastilus, are prostitutes owned by the pimp Lycus. Agorastocles has his clever slave Milphio develop a plan to gain Adelphasium. Milphio instructs Agorastocles to give funds to a certain Collybiscus. Collybiscus will then pretend to go to Lycus and ask to enjoy the pleasures of one of his clients. Then Agorastocles will send someone to claim that the money was stolen from him, and the judgment against Lycus will award Agorastocles the pimp's estate. At the same time, Hanno, a Carthaginian, arrives in Calydon. He is able to identify the two girls as his daughters. He also identifies Agorastocles as his cousin and is happy to permit the wedding of Agorastocles and Adelphasium.

28. Pseudolus (*Pseudolus*) Calidorus is a young Athenian in love. The object of his affection is Phoenicium, a courtesan belonging to the pimp Ballio. Calidorus wishes to purchase Phoenicium, but Ballio—although he vowed he would sell Phoenicium to Calidorus—has reneged, and has instead accepted a deposit for her sale elsewhere. Calidorus enlists the help of his wily slave Pseudolus. Pseudolus plans an intricate campaign that involves getting the money from Calidorus's father, Simo, and cheating Ballio. This plan engages disguises, forged messages, and a wager with Simo. Ultimately, Pseudolus proves successful—the pimp is cheated, Phoenicium and Calidorus are joined, and Pseudolus is feted.

29. Rudens (*The Rope*) During an immense nighttime storm, a ship flounders and sinks. Two young women, Palaestra and Ampelisca, escape the wreck in a small boat and crawl to shore on Cyrene. They are lost, soaking wet, and cold, but make their way to the Temple of Venus where they are provided refuge by the resident priestess. They are the property of Labrax, a pimp who had been convinced to set up shop in Sicily. Meanwhile, a certain older gentleman, Daemones, an Athenian who has retired to Cyrene, has his servants begin cleaning up the debris resulting from the strong winds. At the same time, Plesidippus, a young Athenian gentleman, arrives at Daemones's household inquiring about individuals he had intended to meet at the nearby Temple of Venus. During the cleanup, Grippus, one of Daemones's servants, draws in the sea nets and recovers a trunk of some kind—wreckage from the ship. Believing it may contain gold, he begins thinking about what he may do with it. One of Plesidippus's servants, Trachalio, sees Grippus hauling the trunk to shore, and the two argue about who rightfully owns this package. Daemones, learning that Labrax is attempting to drag Palaestra and Ampelisca out of the temple of Venus, sends his servants to intervene. Ultimately, it is discovered that Labrax had promised to sell Palaestra to Plesidippus, and having taken the fee, had tried to abscond. It is further discovered when the mysterious trunk is opened that Palaestra is in fact the long-lost daughter of Daemones. Father and daughter are reunited and Daemones offers his blessing on a marriage between Palaestra and Plesidippus.

30. Stichus (*Stichus*) Two Athenian sisters, Philumena and Pamphila, miss their husbands and long for their return. The husbands, two brothers, had squandered their fortunes and in an attempt to regain their financial footing have gone abroad, trading. Because they have been gone for three years, the sisters' father, Antipho, has insisted that they remarry, but Philumena and Pamphila, while they wish to be dutiful to their father, remain devoted to their husbands. Ultimately, and rather opportunely, the husbands return, having made their fortune. They are enormously pleased to see their wives, are reconciled with Antipho, and in a celebratory mood they give their servant Stichus a day's freedom and a cask of wine. He gathers some friends together to drink and dance.

31. Trinummus (*The Three Penny Day*) This play focuses on the efforts of an honourable trustee, Callicles, to do the right thing for a young and reckless man and his deserving sister who have been left in his supervision while their father and his friend, Charmides, is away on business. In his father's absence, the young man, Lesbonicus, spends recklessly, and at last puts his father's house on the market to raise funds. Callicles knows that

Charmides, anticipating the need to keep some financial resources hidden from his son, buried treasure within the house. To preserve the treasure without revealing it to the spendthrift Lesbonicus, Callicles purchases the house for a modest amount. This exposes him to criticism, as he is viewed as taking advantage of Lesbonicus. In the meantime, Lysiteles, a citizen of good standing, through the intervention of his father, approaches Lesbonicus to negotiate a match with Charmides's daughter. As the closest relative, Lesbonicus approves of the match, but because he is proud, refuses to let her marry unless she goes with a dowry, and he proposes that the dowry be (what he believes to be) the last remaining portion of his property. Lysiteles, not wanting to beggar the family, declines this offer. Callicles intervenes and, using a portion of the treasure buried in the house, pretends to have gold sent to Lesbonicus from Charmides. Charmides arrives unannounced, however, and when he comes upon a servant alleging to deliver gold to Lesbonicus from him, and then discovering that his house has been sold, determines that he has been betrayed by Callicles. This confusion is ultimately resolved and his daughter and Lysiteles are married, Callicles's trustworthiness is acknowledged and celebrated, Lesbonicus is forgiven for his recklessness, and father and son are reconciled.

32. Truculentus (*Truculentus*) Although this play is named for the surly, truculent servant who attempts to resist the corrupting influence of the female characters, it is really concerned with the devices and stratagems employed by the courtesan Phronesium and her assistant Astaphium as they seduce, entrap, and embezzle funds from a variety of clients. Phronesium has extracted nearly all the material wealth from one of her patrons, Diniarchus, but because he remains infatuated with her, he agrees to hang about and wait for her attention. Two central objects draw Phronesium's notice: Strabax and Stratophanes. Strabax is a bit of a simpleton who is eager to spend his money on the exotic and alluring Phronesium and Astaphium. His servant, Truculentus, attempts to dissuade him from these endeavours and angrily rebuffs Astaphium's advances. Stratophanes and Phronesium had resided together in the past, and Phronesium has developed a plan to extract funds from him. She pretends to be pregnant with Stratophanes's child, and when he arrives to see his young son (she has borrowed a baby), she puts on a great show of having been exhausted by the trials of delivery. He proudly delivers a variety of expensive gifts, but Phronesium disparages these gifts and instead is attentive to the gifts of Diniarchus and Strabax. This provokes a jealous response in Stratophanes, resulting in further gift-giving. In the end, Phronesium and Astaphium prove to be more than a match for all of the men, including the initially reluctant Truculentus.

WORKS BY TERENCE

33. Andria (*The Girl from Andros*) Pamphilus, a young well-to-do Athenian, is secretly in love with Glycerium, an impoverished young woman from Andros. His father, Simo, intends for Pamphilus to marry someone closer to his station in society, his friend Chremes's daughter. But Chremes informs Simo that the wedding cannot go forward because he has discovered that Pamphilus considers Glycerium his wife-to-be. This is shocking news, and to punish and embarrass Pamphilus, Simo announces that the wedding with Chremes's daughter is going forward. He expects that Pamphilus will reveal his scandalous affair, and then Simo—once the affair has been fully exposed—will order him to put Glycerium aside.

It's at this point that Pamphilus consults his most trusted servant, Davos. Davos urges Pamphilus to call his father's bluff and proceed with the sham of a wedding. It will, Davos insists, amount to nothing. Pamphilus does just this. Simo, seeing that Pamphilus means to call his bluff, then hastens to meet with Chremes to attempt to transform the fake wedding into a genuine wedding. Chremes agrees at first but when he discovers that Glycerium has delivered a baby and the father is Pamphilus, he calls the wedding off once more. Luckily, a stranger arrives with information that changes everything. He reveals that Glycerium is a child left in the care of a family of Andros, and in fact is the child of Chremes. At this point, with this new information revealed, Chremes becomes very willing to marry Glycerium to Pamphilus.

34. Adelphoe (*The Brothers*) Following a custom of the times, Demea, the father of two sons, Aeschinus and Ctesipho, elects to separate the boys. He keeps Ctesipho in his household and Aeschinus is sent to be raised by his brother, Micio. Demea and Micio possess two very different temperaments: Demea is strict, Micio permissive. Naturally enough the boys, raised under such different philosophies, grow up manifesting very different attitudes themselves. As they mature, Ctesipho falls in love with a music girl owned by a pimp. Worried that his father will disapprove of their relationship, Ctesipho meets with the music girl covertly. Aeschinus, seeing that his brother desperately loves this girl, breaks into the pimp's home and steals her away. This causes a scandal, and the stricter father, Demea—not knowing on whose behalf Aeschinus has acted—blames his brother for being too permissive with his charge. In the meantime, Aeschinus has developed strong feelings for another young woman, Pamphila, and has promised to marry her. When Sostrato, Pamphila's mother, learns that Aeschinus has raided the pimp's house, she believes that Aeschinus has become attached to the music girl and reneged on his plans to marry Pamphila, and so she publicly upbraids him. Ultimately, Ctesipho is matched and married to the music girl who was carried away from the pimp's house, Aeschinus marries Pamphila, and the two older brothers, Demea and Micio, both learn from one another and cultivate more balanced approaches to life.

35. Eunuchus (*The Eunuch*) Phaedria is an Athenian gentleman desperate for the affection of Thais, a beautiful and clever courtesan. To win her favour, he has purchased two slaves as a gift, one of them a eunuch. He has a rival for her affection, however, a military officer (and a bit of a blowhard) named Thraso, who also has a gift of a sixteen-year-old slave for Thais. Thais is keen to accept Thraso's gift because his slave, Pamphila, was very close to her when she lived in Rhodes. Thais explains to Phaedria that she actually doesn't care for Thraso, but she wishes to free Pamphila—knowing her to be a freeborn girl who was kidnapped—and so will accept Thraso's advances only long enough to receive her gift. Phaedria is disappointed, but agrees to retire to his country estate for two days. Meanwhile, Phaedria's younger brother Chaerea arrives in a state of great excitement, maintaining that he has seen the most beautiful girl he's ever seen—Pamphila. When Chaerea finds out where Pamphila is, he quickly devises a scheme to dress up as the eunuch so that he will be permitted to reside in the house on most intimate terms with Pamphila.

Back at Thais's establishment, Chaerea, disguised as the eunuch, takes advantage of Pamphila, who is understandably distraught. Thais's maids learn that the slave Parmeno assisted Chaerea, and he is told that Chaerea will be castrated as punishment for raping a girl who has turned out to be a freeborn citizen. When Demea arrives—the father of Chaerea and Phaedria, and Parmeno's master—Parmeno has to explain what has happened. Demea rushes into Thais's home and manages to work everything out. Pamphila is reunited with her family, Chaerea is to be married to Pamphila, Phaedria will once more have access to Thais, and even Thraso is not left unsatisfied.

36. Hecyra (*The Mother-in-Law*) One night a young man, Pamphilus, in a state of deep drunkenness rapes a young lady named Philumena. He steals a ring from her hand and later bestows this ring as a gift on a prostitute named Bacchis, who he has a passion for. Philumena is unable to identify the individual who ravished her and is so ashamed of the incident that she keeps it secret. Pamphilus was too drunk, and the night was too dark and consequently, he too is unaware of the identity of the individual he took advantage of. As fate would have it, the parents of Pamphilus arrange a marriage, and the young lady they select is Philumena. After the wedding, Pamphilus is scorned by Bacchis, and he develops a growing respect and attachment for his new wife. While Pamphilus is away on business, Philumena discovers that the rape has resulted in her pregnancy. Anxious that someone may discover what really happened, Philumena returns to her parents' home. Because of Philumena's reluctance to divulge matters pertaining to her rape, there is considerable confusion in the two families about why Philumena has departed her husband's home and speculation rises that there is discord between Philumena and her mother-in-law, Sostrata.

When Pamphilus returns from his business trip, he goes to see his wife, arriving just as she delivers the child. Believing the child to be someone else's, he is once again alienated from his wife. Philumena's mother, Myrrhina, begs Pamphilus to be discrete and not expose Philumena to public scorn. Pamphilus's father, Laches, initially believing that the reason for the discord may be because of some disagreement between Philumena and her mother-in-law, asks that his wife go live out at the country estate, away from the young couple. Then he comes to believe that the discord may be because Pamphilus is still seeing Bacchis. He summons Bacchis to scold her and order her to refrain from meeting with his son. She defends herself, maintaining that she had not had any contact with him since the wedding. He asks her to swear to that in front of Philumena, Myrrhina, and Sostrata. When Bacchis does so, Philumena recognizes the ring that was stolen from her and given to Bacchis and realizes that Pamphilus is in fact the father of the newly born child. This ultimately leads to a reconciliation between Pamphilus and Philumena, and the two interconnected families.

37. Heauton Timorumenos (*The Self Tormentor*) Menedamus is the self-tormentor of this title. He is a father plagued with feelings of guilt because when his son, Clinia, fell in love with a weaver woman's daughter, Antiphila, he chastised the young man. Clinia took the criticism to heart, abandoned Antiphila, left Athens, and went to work as a mercenary in Persia. Regretting his harsh response and the resulting loss of his son, Menedamus moves to a farm outside of Athens where he punishes himself with hard labour day and night. After three months have passed, Chremes, a neighbour, ventures over to invite Menedamus to celebrate the Festival of Bacchus. The two fathers discuss child rearing and Chremes urges Menedamus not to give up hope that his son will return. Menedamus thanks his neighbour for his advice, declines to come and celebrate, and continues working.

In the meantime, Clinia, missing Antiphila but unable to face his father, secretly returns. He connects with his friend, Chremes's son, Clitipho. Clitipho orders his slave Syrus to travel to Athens and fetch Antiphila for Clinia, but when Syrus returns he also brings Clitipho's courtesan, Bacchis with him. Clitipho is concerned that having Bacchis so near to hand will reveal the relationship to his disapproving father. Syrus then enacts a series of strategies to deceive the various fathers, so the sons will escape disapproval. Ultimately, many truths emerge. Antiphila is revealed to be Chremes's daughter, who he had originally urged to be exposed to the elements, but who had been saved by the old weaver woman. Antiphila is permitted to marry Clinia and Clinia is reconciled with his father Menedamus. Chremes first threatens to transfer all of his estate to his newfound daughter, thus leaving Clitipho with nothing, but has a change of heart, and following a candid conversation with his son about the distressing nature of his reckless lifestyle, Clitipho is convinced to put away the courtesan and settle down and marry. Syrus is forgiven for deceiving his master.

38. Phormio (*Phormio*) Two Athenian cousins, Antipho and Phaedria, strive to resolve their complicated situations before their fathers return from travel abroad. Phaedria has become infatuated with an attractive lute player, who is managed by a pimp by the name of Dorio. Phaedria would purchase her, but he's afraid his father would disapprove, and he wasn't left with any money in any case. Antipho has fallen in love with a young orphaned woman that he's certain his father will disapprove of. He turns to his friend Phormio for help. Phormio remembers an obscure law that states that female orphans must be married to the nearest relative. Phormio says he will take Antipho to court, maintain that Antipho is the girl's next of kin, Antipho won't present arguments, and the marriage will fall into place. They do this and Antipho and the girl, Phanium, are married, but Antipho knows his father too well to believe that it will simply end like that.

And it doesn't. The two fathers, Demipho and Chremes return, and Demipho is enraged that his son has married without his consent, and so far beneath his station. Demipho states that he will simply pay the girl a certain dowry equivalency and send her packing. Phormio sees an opportunity and says that he will take the orphaned girl off their hands and marry Phanium if the fee goes to him. Demipho agrees and Phormio swiftly turns about and pays off the pimp on behalf of Phaedria so that he may have the lute player. Ultimately it's learned that Chremes has led a life of bigamy. In addition to having a wife, Nausistrata, in Athens, he's also secretly maintained a wife in Lemnos, and had a daughter by her. That daughter is Phanium, the girl who has married his nephew. Chremes is delighted to learn that what he would have wanted to happen—he had felt under obligation to get his daughter wed—has happened accidentally. He is also simultaneously frightened that with the daughter in town, his wife will learn of his double life. He and Demipho seek to get the funds back from Phormio, but Phormio refuses and when they physically threaten him, he takes the matter to Nausistrata and reveals the other marriage that Chremes had sought to keep hidden. She berates her husband in the strongest terms, applauds Phormio for punishing him and for purchasing the lute player for Phaedria (after all, why shouldn't the boy have this one affair, if her husband can have two wives?). She then promises to befriend Phormio in the future, and invites him to dinner.

BIBLIOGRAPHY/RECOMMENDED WORKS

Afer P. Terentius. Terence. *The Brothers.* Translated by George Colman. U of Adelaide. https://ebooks.adelaide.edu.au/t/terence/adelphoe/complete.html (accessed September 30, 2014).

---. *The Comedies of Terence.* Translated by Frederick Clayton. Exeter, UK: U of Exeter P, 2006.

---. *The Eunuch.* Edited by Henry Thomas Riley. Perseus Digital Library. http://www.perseus.tufts.edu/hopper/text?doc=Perseus:text:1999.02.0114 (accessed August 6, 2014).

---. *Terence: Phormio, The Mother-In-Law, The Brothers.* Edited and translated by John Barsby. Cambridge, MA: Harvard UP, 2001.

Anderson, William S. *Barbarian Play: Plautus' Roman Comedy.* Toronto: U of Toronto P, 1993.

Aristophanes. *The Acharnians.* In *Aristophanes: Four Comedies.* Edited by William Arrowsmith. Translated by Douglass Parker. Ann Arbor, MI: U of Michigan P, 1969.

---. *Aristophanes.* Translated by Benjamin Bickley Rogers. Cambridge, MA: Harvard UP, 1924.

---. *Ecclesiazusae.* Edited and translated by Eugene O'Neill. Perseus Digital Library. www.perseus.tufts.edu/hopper/text?doc=urn:cts:greekLit:tlg0019.tlg010.perseus-eng1 (accessed September 30, 2014).

---. *Lysistrata.* U of Adelaide, Australia. https://ebooks.adelaide.edu.au/a/aristophanes/lysistra/ (accessed September 30, 2014).

---. *The Knights.* Edited by Eugene O'Neill. Perseus Digital Library. http://data.perseus.org/texts/urn:cts:greekLit:tlg0019.tlg002.perseus-eng1 (accessed September 30, 2014).

---. *Peace.* Edited by Eugene O'Neill Jr. Perseus Digital Library. http://www.perseus.tufts.edu/hopper/text?doc=Perseus:text:1999.01.0038 (accessed August 6, 2014).

---. *Peace*. Edited by Daniel Stevenson. Project Gutenberg, 2008. http://www.gutenberg
.org/files/2571/2571-h/2571-h.htm (accessed August 6, 2014).

---. *The Frogs*. The Internet Classics Archive. http://classics.mit.edu/Aristophanes/frogs
.pl.txt (accessed August 6, 2014).

---. *Thesmophoriazusae*. Edited by Eugene O'Neill Jr. Perseus Digital Library. http://
www.perseus.tufts.edu/hopper/text?doc=Perseus:text:1999.01.0042 (accessed August
6, 2014).

---. *The Wasps*. Edited by Eugene O'Neill Jr. Perseus Digital Library. http://www.perseus
.tufts.edu/hopper/text?doc=Perseus:text:1999.01.0044 (accessed August 6, 2014).

Aristotle. *Aristotle's Poetics*. Edited by John Baxter. Translated by George Whalley.
Montreal: McGill-Queen's UP, 1997.

Arnot, Peter D., ed. and trans. *Two Classical Comedies*. New York: Meredith
Corporation, 1958.

Arrowsmith, William, ed. *Aristophanes: Four Comedies*. Ann Arbor, MI: U of Michigan
P, 1994.

Balme, Maurice. *Menander: The Plays and Fragments*. New York: Oxford UP, 2001.

Barsby, John. *Terence: The Eunuch, Phormio, The Brothers*. Bristol: Bristol
Classical, 1991.

Beacham, Richard C. *The Roman Theatre and Its Audience*. Cambridge, MA: Harvard
UP, 1991.

Bergson, Henri. *Laughter*. Translated by Cloudesley Shovell Henry Brereton and Fred
Rothwell. New York: Macmillan, 1928.

Brandt, J. Rasmus, and Jon W. Iddeng, eds. *Greek and Roman Festivals: Content,
Meaning, and Practice*. Oxford Scholarship Online, 2013. http://www
.oxfordscholarship.com/view/10.1093/acprof:oso/9780199696093.001.0001
/acprof-9780199696093?rskey=B17DVV&result=1 (accessed August 6, 2014).

Brown, Peter, ed. *Terence: The Comedies*. New York: Oxford UP, 2006.

Calder, Andrew. *Molière: The Theory and Practice of Comedy*. London: Continuum, 2000.

Cooke, Thomas. *Terence's Comedies Translated into English with Critical and
Explanatory Notes*. London: J. Bartley and T. Cox, 1734.

Corrigan, Robert W. *Comedy: Meaning and Form*. San Francisco: Chandler, 1965.

Csapo, Eric. *Actors and Icons of the Ancient Theater*. Hoboken, NJ: Wiley-Blackwell, 2010.

Denard, Hugh. "Lost Theatre and Performance Traditions in Greece and Italy." In *The Cambridge Companion to Greek and Roman Theatre*. Edited by Marianne McDonald and J. Michael Walton. New York: Cambridge UP, 2007.

Duckworth, George E. *The Nature of Roman Comedy*, 2nd ed. Norman: U of Oklahoma P, 1994.

Easterling, Pat, and Edith Hall, eds. *Greek and Roman Actors: Aspects of an Ancient Profession.* Cambridge, UK: Cambridge UP, 2002.

Fantham, Elaine. *Roman Readings: Roman Response to Greek Literature from Plautus to Statius and Quintilian.* Berlin: Walter de Gruyter, 2011.

Feibleman, James Kern. *In Praise of Comedy: A Study in Its Theory and Practice.* New York: Russell and Russell, 1962.

Fontaine, Michael. *Funny Words in Plautine Comedy.* Oxford Scholarship Online, 2009. http://www.oxfordscholarship.com/view/10.1093/acprof:oso/9780195341447.001.0001/acprof-9780195341447 (accessed August 6, 2014).

Fortson, Benjamin W. *Language and Rhythm in Plautus.* Berlin: Walter de Gruyter, 2008.

Freud, Sigmund. "Jokes and the Comic." In *Jokes and Their Relation to the Unconscious.* Edited and translated by James Strachey. New York: W.W. Norton, 1960.

Freydberg, Bernard. *Philosophy and Comedy: Aristophanes, Logos, and Eros.* Bloomington: Indiana UP, 2008.

Handley, E.W. *Menander and Plautus: A Study in Comparison.* London: University College London, 1968.

Hobbes, Thomas. *Leviathan.* Project Gutenberg, 2009. http://www.gutenberg.org/files/3207/3207-h/3207-h.htm (accessed August 6, 2014).

Karavas, Orestis, and Jean-Luc Vix. "On the Reception of Menander in the Imperial Period." In *Menander in Contexts.* Edited by Alan H. Sommerstein. New York: Routledge, 2013.

Konstan, David. *Greek Comedy and Ideology.* New York: Oxford UP, 1995.

Levin, Harry. *Playboys and Killjoys: An Essay on the Theory and Practice of Comedy.* Toronto: Oxford UP, 1988.

Matthews, Brander. *The Development of the Drama.* New York: Charles Scribner's Sons, 1912.

McDonald, Marianne, and Michael J. Walton, eds. *The Cambridge Companion to Greek and Roman Theatre.* New York: Cambridge UP, 2007.

McGlew, James F. *Citizens on Stage: Comedy and Political Culture in the Athenian Democracy*. Ann Arbor, MI: U of Michigan P, 2005.

Menander. *The Bad Tempered Man*. In *The Plays and Fragments*. Translated by Maurice Balme. Oxford: Oxford UP, 2001.

---. *The Girl from Samos*. In *The Plays and Fragments*. Translated by Maurice Balme. Oxford: Oxford UP, 2001.

---. *Menander*. Edited by David R. Slavitt and Palmer Bovie. Philadelphia: U of Pennsylvania P, 1998.

Miola, Robert S. *Shakespeare and Classical Comedy: The Influence of Plautus and Terence*. Oxford Scholarship Online, 2011. http://www.oxfordscholarship.com/view/10.1093 /acprof:oso/9780198182696.001.0001/acprof-9780198182696?rskey=WRLpsx&result=1 (accessed August 6, 2014).

Moore, Timothy J. *The Theater of Plautus: Playing to the Audience*. Austin: U of Texas P, 1998.

O'Bryhim, Shawn, ed. *Greek and Roman Comedy: Translations and Interpretations of Four Representative Plays*. Austin: U of Texas P, 2001.

Parker, Douglass. Introduction to *The Acharnians*. In *Aristophanes: Four Comedies*. Edited by William Arrowsmith. Ann Arbor, MI: U of Michigan P, 1969.

Plautus, Titus Maccius. *The Brothers Menaechmus*. Edited by Henry Thomas Riley. Perseus Digital Library. www.perseus.tufts.edu/hopper/text?doc=urn:cts :latinLit:phi0119.phi010.perseus-eng1 (accessed September 30, 2014).

---. *Captivi: The Captives*. Edited by Henry Thomas Riley. Perseus Digital Library. http://www.perseus.tufts.edu/hopper/text?doc=Perseus:text:1999.02.0096 (accessed August 6, 2014).

---. *Casina*. Edited by F. Leo. Perseus Digital Library. http://www.perseus.tufts.edu /hopper/text?doc=Perseus:text:1999.02.0035 (accessed August 6, 2014).

---. *Casina*. Edited by Henry Thomas Riley. Perseus Digital Library. http://www.perseus .tufts.edu/hopper/text?doc=Perseus:text:1999.02.0097 (accessed August 6, 2014).

---. *Plautus: The Comedies*, vol. 1, 2, 3, & 4. Edited by David R. Slavitt and Palmer Bovie. Baltimore: Johns Hopkins UP, 1995.

---. *Epidicus*. Edited by Henry Thomas Riley. Perseus Digital Library. http://data .perseus.org/citations/urn:cts:latinLit:phi0119.phi009.perseus-eng1:intro.1 (accessed August 6, 2014).

---. *Miles Gloriosus*. Edited by Henry Thomas Riley. Perseus Digital Library. www.perseus.tufts.edu/hopper/text?doc=urn:cts:latinLit:phi0119.phi012 .perseus-eng1 (accessed September 30, 2014).

---. *The Persian*. Edited by Henry Thomas Riley. Perseus Digital Library. http://www .perseus.tufts.edu/hopper/text?doc=Perseus:text:1999.02.0105 (accessed August 6, 2014).

---. *The Pot of Gold*. In *Plautus: The Comedies*, vol. 2. Edited by David R. Slavitt and Palmer Bovie. Baltimore: Johns Hopkins UP, 1995.

---. *Pseudolus*. Edited by Henry Thomas Riley. Perseus Digital Library. http://data .perseus.org/citations/urn:cts:latinLit:phi0119.phi016.perseus-eng1:intro.subject (accessed August 6, 2014).

---. *The Two Bacchises*. Translated by Paul Dixon. Project Gutenberg, 2005. www.gutenberg.org/files/16564/16564-h/16564-h.htm#Bacchides (accessed September 30, 2014).

Potts, L.J. "The Subject Matter of Comedy." In *Comedy, Meaning and Form*. Edited by Robert W. Corrigan. San Francisco: Chandler, 1965.

Radice, Betty. *Terence: The Brothers and Other Plays*. New York: Penguin, 1965.

Robson, James. *Aristophanes: An Introduction*. London: Bloomsbury, 2009.

Roselli, David Kawalko. *Theater of the People: Spectators and Society in Ancient Athens*. Austin: U of Texas P, 2011.

Segal, Erich. *Roman Laughter: The Comedy of Plautus*. New York: Oxford UP, 1987.

Slater, Niall W. *Plautus in Performance*. Princeton: Princeton UP, 1985.

Smith, Peter, ed. and trans. *Plautus: Three Comedies*. Ithaca: Cornell UP, 1991.

Smith, Willard Mallalieu. *The Nature of Comedy*. Boston: Gorham Press, 1930.

Sommerstein, Alan H, ed. *Menander in Contexts*. New York: Routledge, 2013.

Sophocles. *Antigone*. Greek Texts. http://www.greektexts.com/library/Sophocles /Antigone/eng/index.html (accessed August 6, 2014).

Stott, Andrew. Comedy. New York: Routledge, 2004.

Sutton, Dana F. *Ancient Comedy: The War of the Generations*. Toronto: Macmillan, 1993.

Walbank, F.W. *The Cambridge Ancient History*. Cambridge: Cambridge UP, 1984.

ACKNOWLEDGEMENTS

I would like to acknowledge the Writers' Trust of Canada's great gift in providing me with the time and space to work on this book. While I was in residence at the Pierre Berton House in Dawson City, I was able to consider all the many separate elements of Greek and Roman comedy, make connections between them, and write. For this gesture of generosity I am very grateful.

I am also grateful to the broad community of scholars, translators, and lovers of ancient literature for their passionate interest in the comic writings of the early Greek and Roman civilizations, and the many essays, critical analyses, and texts they have written.

And, as always, I am immensely grateful to my wife and family for their interest, patience, and support as I developed this project.

Clem Martini is an award-winning playwright, novelist, and screenwriter with over thirty plays and nine books of fiction and non-fiction to his credit, including *Bitter Medicine: A Graphic Memoir of Mental Illness*, winner of the Calgary Book Award, and his most recent anthology of plays, *Martini With A Twist*. He has served on the boards of numerous writing organizations including the Alberta Playwrights Network, the Playwrights Guild of Canada, and the Canadian Creative Writers and Writing Programs. His texts on playwriting, *The Blunt Playwright* and *The Greek Playwright*, are used in universities and colleges across the country. He is currently a professor in the School of Creative and Performing Arts at the University of Calgary.

First edition: December 2014
Printed and bound in Canada by Marquis Book Printing, Montreal

Cover design by Blake Sproule

PLAYWRIGHTS
CANADA PRESS

202-269 Richmond Street West
Toronto, ON
M5V 1X1

416.703.0013
info@playwrightscanada.com
playwrightscanada.com

RECYCLED
Paper made from
recycled material
FSC® C103567

Printed on Enviro 100% post-consumer EcoLogo certified paper,
processed chlorine free and manufactured using biogas energy.